METRO-LAND

1924 edition
with a new introduction from
Oliver Green

southbank
publishing

Metro-Land (1924 edition)

This facsimile edition published 2004

Southbank Publishing
21 Great Ormond Street
London WC1N 3JB

www.southbankpublishing.com

A CIP catalogue record for this book is available from the
British Library.

ISBN – 1 904915 00 0

2 4 6 8 10 9 7 5 3 1

INTRODUCTION

A detail of a decorative poster map of the British Empire Exhibition at
Wembley issued by the Underground Group in 1924. Cartography by
Thomas Derrick, illustration by Edward Bawden.

AN INTRODUCTION TO METRO-LAND

Metro-land is the creation of the Metropolitan Railway's Publicity Department. The title was devised as a catchy marketing brand name for the areas north west of London in Middlesex, Hertfordshire and Buckinghamshire served by the line. It first appeared in print in 1915 with the publication of *Metro-land*, a guidebook designed to promote the area for leisure excursion travel from London. More significantly, *Metro-land* was intended to stimulate new residential development, populating these districts with middle-class commuters who would travel to and from London daily on the Metropolitan's services. Launching a promotion like this during the First World War, when house-hunting was hardly a priority for many people, does not look like the best of timing. But the essence of the scheme was to blossom into a huge success in the post-war twenties, when new suburban house sales around London took off as never before. The 1924 edition of *Metro-land* reproduced here was published just as the boom was under way.

A new edition of *Metro-land* was published annually from 1915 until 1932, the last full year of the Metropolitan's existence as an independent railway company. On 1 July 1933, the Met unwillingly became part of London

Early Metro-land promotion in action. Two of the Metropolitan's wartime women workers posting *Metro-land* advertisements outside a rival company's station (Cricklewood, Midland Railway) c 1917.

Transport, the new authority that took over all bus, tram and underground railway services in the London area. The Metropolitan was downgraded from main line railway status to just one of London Transport's seven underground lines. Metro-land was dropped immediately from the advertising vocabulary of the new Board, never to be used again in official publicity, although London's suburban growth continued until it was ended abruptly by the outbreak of war in September 1939.

Metro-land may have lost its official standing only eighteen years after its invention, but the name had already entered the language as an almost generic expression of suburban life. A popular song called *My Little Metro-land Home* had been published in 1920. The word had even, through Evelyn Waugh's fictional character Margot Metroland, appeared for the first time in the pages of a novel (*Decline and Fall*, published in 1928). Metro-land's characteristics were later to be affectionately evoked in the poems of John Betjeman, such as *The Metropolitan Railway* (1954) and in his nostalgic BBC television programme, *Metro-land*, made in 1973. Yet another perspective appears in Julian Barnes' first novel, *Metroland* (1980), where the writer draws on memories of his own suburban upbringing in the area in the 1960s. For Barnes, 'Metro-land is a country with elastic borders which every visitor can draw for himself, as Stevenson drew his map of Treasure Island'. In little more than half a century, Metro-land grew from being an ad man's creative invention into a more prosaic reality in the 1920s and 30s, a wistful post-war recollection from the 1950s onwards and finally a new land of personal imagination by 1980.

The area that was christened Metro-land in 1915 had been opened up by the railway between 1880 and 1905. In the process, the Metropolitan was itself transformed from a short urban underground feeder line linking three London

An early edition of *Metro-land* c 1916.

termini with the City, into a fully fledged long distance railway with main line aspirations. The original section of the Metropolitan, opened in January 1863 between Paddington and Farringdon, was the world's first underground railway. It was gradually extended over the next twenty years until, by linking up at both ends with London's second main underground line, the District Railway, the Inner Circle (now the Circle line) was completed in 1884. By this time, the Metropolitan was concentrating its resources on promoting a potentially more lucrative expansion out into the country through London's north west suburbs. This began as a modest branch line from Baker Street to Swiss Cottage, originally called the Metropolitan and St. John's Wood Railway, which opened in 1868. The railway was then pushed overground through green fields on the edge of London, beyond Finchley Road to Willesden Green (1879), Harrow (1880), Pinner (1885), Rickmansworth (1887) and Chesham (1889). Chesham became a branch terminus when the main line was built onwards from Chalfont Road (now Chalfont and Latimer) through Amersham to Aylesbury (1892). A link with the existing Aylesbury and Buckingham Railway took Metropolitan trains on to Verney Junction, a remote country station in north Buckinghamshire, where there were connecting services on other lines to Banbury, Bletchley and Oxford.

Through Metropolitan services from Verney Junction to Baker Street were introduced in 1897. A short branch from Quainton Road to Brill, built by the Duke of Buckingham to serve his private estate, was also acquired by the Metropolitan in 1899. Thus, by the turn of the century, the Metropolitan's domain stretched over more than fifty miles from central London through the Chilterns into deepest Bucks. At the time, this was less about preparing the ground for suburban development than the initial building blocks of a far grander plan by the company chairman, Sir Edward Watkin. His ambition was to make the Metropolitan the key link in a main line network running from Manchester via London to Dover, then through a proposed Channel tunnel to Paris and the rest of Continental Europe. This was no idle dream. Watkin was already chairman of two other existing railway companies along the route as well as the nascent Manchester, Sheffield and Lincolnshire Railway, which was planning a new trunk line from the north west to London. He was one of the most powerful and influential of the late Victorian railway barons, but a debilitating stroke forced him to resign as Metropolitan chairman in 1894. The company's more grandiose and visionary plans effectively collapsed with him. Although the successful completion of a Channel rail tunnel was still a century away, other more modest development possibilities were already emerging for the Metropolitan.

As was often the case when a new railway opened, the Metropolitan's Extension Line brought new residential development in its wake, although not always as quickly as the company would have liked. Unlike any other railway, however, the Metropolitan became directly involved in housing development itself, using surplus land alongside the line bought before the railway was built. Property not required for railway purposes was usually resold when construction was complete, but the Metropolitan cannily hung on to its purchases. The company's first property development venture was the Willesden Park Estate, laid out on railway land near Willesden Green station in the 1880s and 1890s. The houses were modest, semi-detached villas intended for rental by middle-class families.

Another two housing estates, including some rather more upmarket residences, were begun in the early 1900s further down the line at Pinner (Cecil Park) and at Wembley Park, where a large area of land south of the railway had been acquired in 1890 to develop as sports and pleasure grounds. This was another Watkin scheme that included, as its centrepiece, plans for a massive viewing tower inspired by the success of the Eiffel Tower, built for the Paris Exhibition of 1889. The Wembley Park pleasure grounds were opened to the public in 1894, served by a new station, but the great tower had already run into financial and construction difficulties. It never rose above the first 155ft. high stage, a mere fifth of its intended stature. Without the main attraction, the hoped for crowds of trippers arriving on Metropolitan trains never materialised. Watkin's Folly, as the part built tower became known, was eventually closed to visitors and finally demolished in 1907. Wembley had yet to become a household name.

During the Edwardian years, the ground was laid for the full-scale development of Metro-land that took place in the 1920s. The railway service was further extended and modernised with a new branch line from Harrow to Uxbridge, opened in 1904, and the start of electric services the following year over the inner sections of the Metropolitan and as far out as Uxbridge. Banishing steam locomotives from passenger trains on the Met's sub-surface lines was not before time, as the unpleasant atmosphere of its stations and tunnels compared badly with the clean new

Opening day special train on the Uxbridge branch at Ruislip. 30 June 1904. Public services began on 4 July using steam trains for the first six months. This locomotive, Met no. 1, is preserved in working order at the Buckinghamshire Railway Centre at Quainton.

rival electric Tube railways that were criss-crossing the capital. A sign of the new standards to which the company aspired was the introduction of two Pullman cars in 1910. These were used on some of the fast long-distance services to and from Buckinghamshire, providing drinks and light refreshments to first-class passengers paying a supplementary fare. Tea or coffee with buttered toast, cake and jam was available for 1s 6d (7½p), while a light breakfast, lunch or supper cost 3s 0d (15p). A full range of alcoholic drinks was also available from the bar.

Two luxury Pullman cars named *Mayflower* and *Galatea* were introduced on some long distance Met services in June 1910. This is the opulent interior of one of them.

Such luxuries were only taken up by a small proportion of the Metropolitan's clientele. The Pullman service was more of an image builder than a profit maker, but other more significant improvements that could be appreciated and experienced by all the railway's customers were being developed in this period. This was particularly true after the appointment of Robert Hope Selbie as General Manager in 1908. It was the autocratic but far-sighted Selbie who now drove a series of new initiatives for the Met and who would oversee the successful creation of Metro-land. Selbie recognised that promotion of new traffic for the railway had to go hand in hand with visibly improved services. A major investment in additional express tracks over the busy bottleneck section between Finchley Road and Wembley Park during 1913–15 was a prime example of this. Selbie's additional proposals, to extend the electrification of the main line beyond Harrow to Rickmansworth and to build a new electric branch to Watford, had to be postponed with the outbreak of war in 1914. Further estate development was

also brought to a temporary halt, although the optimistic launch of the first *Metro-land* guide only a year later showed that the railway had not shelved all its plans for the duration of the war.

In January 1919, only two months after the Armistice, a scheme was announced to create a new property company that would manage and develop the railway's land holdings. Until this point, the commercial administration of the Met's estates had been

The 1920 edition of *Metro-land*.

in the hands of the Surplus Lands Committee. The Committee's responsibilities were now taken over by Metropolitan Railway Country Estates Ltd. Legally it was a separate company independent of the railway, but in practice the MRCE was under the control of the Metropolitan's directors. Selbie, who was an MRCE director from the start, became a director of the Metropolitan Railway in 1922 whilst continuing to serve as its General Manager. It was a cosy arrangement that gave the Metropolitan the unique opportunity among railway companies to become a profitable property developer.

Between 1919 and 1933, the MRCE developed a series of private housing estates all down the line at Neasden, Wembley Park, Northwick Park, Eastcote, Rayners Lane, Ruislip, Hillingdon, Pinner, Rickmansworth, Chorleywood and Amersham. In the early days, the estates company built some houses itself, but the usual pattern was to lay out an estate and then sell plots to individual purchasers wishing to have a house built to their own specifications. Later on, the design and construction was usually undertaken by other companies who would offer the prospective purchaser a choice of house sizes and styles at a range of prices. The procedure is described on pages 80 to 95.

A poster promoting the 1926 edition of *Metro-land*.

The annual *Metro-land* guide was always the main advertising medium for these developments. The seductive dream of a new home on the edge of beautiful countryside but with every modern convenience, including a fast rail service to central London, was an appealing vision eighty years ago, and remains so today. In true advertising tradition, the Met's copywriters went way over the top in their purple prose, trying rather unconvincingly to blend notions of age-old rural tradition with civilised progress: 'This is a good parcel of English soil in which to build home and strike root, inhabited from of old ... the new settlement

RAMBLES IN METRO-LAND

A NEW SERIES OF FOUR BOOKLETS CONTAINING CAREFULLY DRAWN ROUTE MAPS AND CONCISE DIRECTIONS OF 68 CHARMING RAMBLES IN METRO-LAND AGGREGATING NEARLY 600 MILES, NOW OBTAINABLE, PRICE 2ᵈ EACH, AT ANY METRO. BOOKING OFFICE OR BOOKSTALL

Poster advertising the Met's Country Walks booklets, mainly featuring rambles from the outer Metro-land stations beyond Amersham, 1929.

of Metro-land proceeds apace; the new colonists thrive amain'. The language must have sounded contrived even then, although a quick glance today at the ads and features in the weekly *Homes and Property* supplement of the London *Evening Standard* will show that marketing methods have only changed superficially. Lifestyle advertising and promotion using fashionable jargon still seems to work. *Metro-land* was just one of the first and most successful examples of an approach to property marketing that is now familiar to us all.

Until after the First World War, hardly anyone in Britain owned their own home. Before 1914, even the wealthier middle classes usually rented, but in the 1920s actually buying a new house with a mortgage became a practical possibility for thousands of people. Building societies, which provided most of the new mortgages for house purchases, did not require large cash deposits and loan rates were low. One of the fastest growing societies in the London area which helped finance the Metro-land boom was the Abbey Road, later to become the Abbey National, which registered a 700% increase in borrowers between 1926 and 1936. A prominent advertisement for the Abbey appears in this and most subsequent editions of *Metro-land*.

Every *Metro-land* booklet features evocative descriptions and photographs of historic villages and rural vistas in what its authors claimed to be 'London's nearest countryside … where charm and peace await you'. Production and printing were of an exceptionally high quality, with the special luxury, for this period, of coloured covers and plates that could be ordered in sets for framing. No doubt the brochure conjured up a tempting prospect for the hiker or day tripper, but *Metro-land's* real target market was always the prospective resident rather than the casual visitor. Selbie and his colleagues always had new season ticket holders in their sights. In the persuasive words of the 1920 edition of *Metro-land*, 'the strain which the London business or professional man has to undergo amidst the turmoil and bustle of Town can only be counteracted by the quiet restfulness and comfort of a residence amidst pure air and surroundings, and whilst jaded vitality and taxed nerves are the natural penalties of modern conditions, Nature has, in the delightful districts abounding in Metro-land, placed a potential remedy at hand'.

As well as offering a guide to visitors and potential residents of Metro-land itself (the outer suburban and country area starting at Wembley), this *Metro-land* booklet purports to offer guidance to anyone travelling up to Town with a 'How to get about London section' on pages 25 to 34. Closer inspection reveals the bizarre recommendation that visitors start by memorising the position of the most convenient railway station for their destination (p28) linked to the misleading suggestion that as the Metropolitan 'goes north, south, east and west', there is always likely to be a Met station or interchange with the Tube close at hand. The Key Plans on pages 32 and 33 actually give a rather poor indication of the precise street locations of many central London Tube stations, which almost suggests a deliberate attempt to sabotage any use of rival Underground services. It is also curious that the photographs of the City on pages 30 and 31 are more than a decade out of date. They were clearly taken around 1910 when there were still horse buses on the streets. Is this a sly dig at another rival transport company, the London General Omnibus Company, which had in fact replaced its entire horse drawn fleet with new motor buses in 1911? If this is simply an oversight, it gives the photographs a strangely archaic feel, particularly alongside a text which is obsessively fixated on the modern features and up to the minute statistics of the Met's new services to the forthcoming British Empire Exhibition at Wembley. Perhaps the simple explanation is that this 1924 edition of *Metro-land* has been rather uncomfortably adapted to squeeze in as much as possible about the new show at Wembley as this was clearly about to be the dominant attraction of the area in the year ahead.

The British Empire Exhibition of 1924/25 not only put Wembley permanently on the map, but acted as a timely boost for Metro-land as a whole. It was not a project originally promoted by the Metropolitan Railway, but the fortuitous choice of Wembley Park as the site led to considerable benefits for the railway and the area. The exhibition was the largest to be held in this country since the Great Exhibition of 1851 in Hyde Park. Its purpose was to promote both the image and economy of the Empire, or in the words of the official guidebook, 'to display the natural resources of the Empire, and the activities, industrial and social, of their peoples'. The Metropolitan was the first to profit from the venture through the sale of 216 acres of Wembley Park to the exhibition company in January 1922, at last recouping some of Watkin's ill-fated investment of the 1890s.

Metropolitan Railway poster for the first cup final at Wembley, 1923.

The first physical manifestation of the new scheme was, appropriately enough, erected on the site of Watkin's Tower. This was a huge national sports arena, the largest of its kind in the world, built almost entirely with the newly refined construction technique of reinforced concrete. The Empire Stadium could accommodate 125,000 spectators and, as the promoters were keen to emphasise, was one and a half times the size of that earlier classical arena of empire, the Coliseum in Rome. Wembley Stadium was first used to stage the FA Cup Final on 28 April 1923 when Bolton Wanderers beat West Ham 2–0. The match nearly had to be abandoned before kick-off when the over-capacity crowd spilled past the barriers and on to the pitch. A potentially dangerous situation was skilfully averted in the famous 'white horse incident', a

One of the Metropolitan's fleet of 20 powerful new electric locomotives on display at the Wembley Exhibition in 1925.

successfully improvised crowd control manoeuvre led by a single mounted policeman who slowly circled the touch line, easing the fans back until the pitch was clear. Without making any direct reference to this incident, *Metro-land's* copywriter boasts on page 31 that the Met carried 152,000 passengers to Wembley Park on Cup Final day, depositing them 'at the amazing rate of a thousand a minute'. If this is correct, the Met alone brought in thousands more fans than the stadium could accommodate and contributed directly to the chaotic situation, which hardly seems an achievement to celebrate!

The giant twin towers of the stadium, one of which features on the cover of this edition of *Metro-land,* came to symbolise Wembley as the national home of English football. They stood for eighty years until the controversial but long overdue redevelopment of the site by the Football Association finally began in 2003, and the demolition crews moved in. The various great ferro-concrete Palaces and Pavilions of the Empire Exhibition described here, and the adjacent Amusements Park, were ready for a grand royal inauguration by King George V on 23 April 1924 (St. George's Day). The King's speech was relayed by the BBC, then just eighteen months old and still a tiny company, not a national corporation, to nearly seven million listeners who for the first time heard a monarch's actual voice over the wireless. The exhibition organisers confidently predicted at least 25 million visitors to 'Wonderful Wembley'. In fact, 17.4 million people had passed through the turnstiles by the end of the exhibition on 1 November. It was decided to re-open Wembley for a second season in 1925 with various new exhibits. Inevitably it was less popular, attracting 9.7 million customers, though even this total looks impressive when compared with the ill-fated Millennium Dome exhibition at Greenwich in 2000, which was visited by only 6.5 million people in 12 months, just over half the projected target figure.

A comparison of the census returns for 1921 and 1931 shows a population increase of nearly 11% for Greater London as a whole, with a much higher rate of growth in the north west suburbs between five and ten miles from the centre. The Metro-land districts of Harrow, Ruislip-Northwood, Uxbridge and Wembley all experienced increases of more than 50%. In 1929, the Metropolitan Railway's Commercial Manager estimated that between 1919 and 1928, some 12,000 houses had been built within half a mile of the stations between Willesden

Metro-land triumphant. A Metropolitan poster of 1929 reflecting the company's success at boosting its commuter market.

Green, Uxbridge and Watford and that a further 17,000 were planned.

Just as the railway company hoped, the rapid development of Metro-land in the 1920s created a significant rise in ticket sales, and particularly of seasons, although the growth rate varied considerably. Comparing figures for monthly season tickets issued at individual stations in 1921 with 1928, for example, Aylesbury and Chorleywood remained almost constant, but at Rickmansworth, Ruislip and Ruislip Manor, sales nearly doubled, and at Preston Road, Northwick Park and Wembley Park, the rise was more than 700%. The most spectacular growth of all was at Ickenham, where only 59 monthly tickets were sold in 1921, compared to 1,497 in 1928.

Even the doorplates of Metropolitan carriages reflected the Metro-land message.

Some of the shelved pre-war modernisation plans were implemented in this period to help meet and further stimulate growing traffic demand. Apart from the temporary boost of the Wembley Exhibition in 1924/5 and the other special events like the Cup Final from 1923, this was nearly all commuter based. The extension of electric working to Rickmansworth and construction of a new branch to Watford were both completed in 1925. Baker Street station, the hub and headquarters of the Metropolitan, often described in the company's publicity as 'the gateway to Metro-land', had been partly rebuilt just before the war. Plans for a grand hotel over the station changed into a scheme for a giant block of flats, Chiltern Court, completed in 1929. HG Wells and Arnold Bennett were among the first tenants of what was claimed by *Metroland* to be the largest and most luxurious apartment block in London, opening 'a new chapter in residential flat technique'.

LIVE ON
THE
WELLER
ESTATE
AMERSHAM

The Metropolitan's last major infrastructure project was another new branch line from Wembley Park to Stanmore, which was

A sales brochure for the last of the Metro-land housing estates at Amersham, started in 1930.

opened in December 1932 (later to become part of the Bakerloo line in 1939 and finally the Jubilee line in 1979). Yet more suburban development followed in the mid-1930s around the new stations on this branch, notably at Kingsbury and Queensbury. The last and furthest flung of the MRCE's own housing developments, the Weller Estate at Amersham, was started in 1930 and eventually comprised 535 semi-detached houses and 51 shops. A year earlier, an even larger development christened Harrow Garden Village had got under way at Rayners Lane, and in just a few years, what had been a remote country halt on the Uxbridge line with only a few farm buildings nearby was a busy rebuilt station surrounded by shopping parades, a spectacular art deco cinema and new suburban streets lined with semis.

In some respects, the heyday of Metro-land was over by the early 1930s. Season ticket sales on the Metropolitan reached a peak in 1930, then started to decline as the effects of the economic slump began to bite even in the prosperous south east. Unrestricted development, in the boom years of the 1920s, had already transformed many of these districts very rapidly from open countryside to drab and monotonous suburban sprawl. The notion of Metro-land as a 'rural

One of the Metropolitan's Country Walks booklets, 1929. The cover photograph shows old Wendover, not greatly changed today.

Arcadia' no longer matched the suburban reality of Wembley Park or Rayners Lane, although the outer areas

A 1929 poster advertising the new Metro-land housing development on the farmland around Rayners Lane station, which was promoted as Harrow Garden Village.

beyond Rickmansworth still retained their country character and have done so to this day. Many of the country walks suggested in *Metro-land* and other Met publications from eighty years ago are largely unchanged. A weekend stroll over Coombe Hill and past the Prime Minister's country residence at Chequers or along the River Chess from Latimer village is still through beautiful unspoilt countryside and can be highly recommended. The High Street in old Amersham pictured on page 68 is always full of cars today, but otherwise the buildings and streetscape have been carefully preserved; similarly, the description of old Wendover on page 75 could have been written last week.

Metro-land has always been infused with contradiction and paradox. In opening up 'London's nearest countryside' to thousands of new residents, it was inevitable that much of that land would not remain rural for long. This was a process of both creation and destruction that offered real benefits and a new life to many people even if it was ridiculously oversold. But allowing the process to continue virtually unregulated was not sustainable. In the end, the apparently remorseless outward spread of suburban London was only brought to a halt by the war in 1939. After the war, new development was effectively curtailed by the imposition of the Green Belt and other planning restrictions. As a result, much of Metro-land has remained virtually as it was at the outbreak of war, forever marooned in the 1930s, and some of what had been created in the previous twenty years has since been listed or declared conservation areas. Many people still find this difficult to understand and see little merit in Metro-land, but even those who can't stand the suburbs would surely agree that this curious early twentieth century phenomenon deserves our attention.

This edition of *Metro-land* is full of the brash, confident optimism of the 1920s. It may be misleading and inaccurate as a historical document but that is also part of its fascination and charm. Enjoy it for its quirky character. Those readers wanting to explore the history of Metro-land and the Metropolitan Railway further are recommended to turn first to Alan A Jackson's exhaustively researched and near definitive books *London's Metropolitan Railway* (David and Charles, 1986), *Semi-Detached London* (Wild Swan, 1991) and his forthcoming *London's Metro-land* (Capital Transport, 2005). Photographs, original Met publications, including copies of *Metro-land*, and even a very early silent film made for the Metropolitan Railway in 1911, showing a trip down the line, can be consulted at London's Transport Museum in Covent Garden (Tel. 0207 379 6344 and www.ltmuseum.co.uk for details).

Oliver Green
Head Curator
London's Transport Museum

METRO-LAND

BRITISH EMPIRE EXHIBITION NUMBER

Containing a

**GENERAL DESCRIPTION OF THE
BRITISH EMPIRE EXHIBITION**

HOW TO GET ABOUT LONDON

and a

**COMPREHENSIVE & DESCRIPTIVE
:   :   REVIEW OF THE   :   :
VARIOUS DISTRICTS SERVED BY
THE METROPOLITAN RAILWAY**

Baker Street Station,
London, N.W.1

R. H. SELBIE,
General Manager

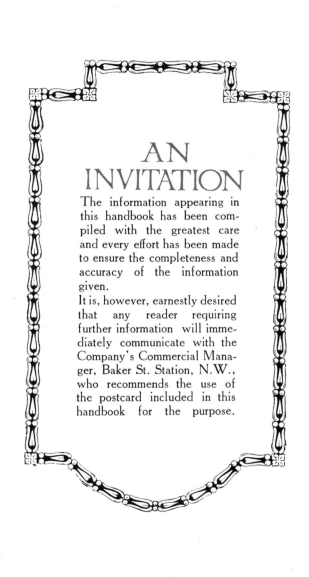

AN
INVITATION

The information appearing in this handbook has been compiled with the greatest care and every effort has been made to ensure the completeness and accuracy of the information given.

It is, however, earnestly desired that any reader requiring further information will immediately communicate with the Company's Commercial Manager, Baker St. Station, N.W., who recommends the use of the postcard included in this handbook for the purpose.

THE FALLS, CHESSWATER HOUSE, RICKMANSWORTH.

PLATE II

CONTENTS.

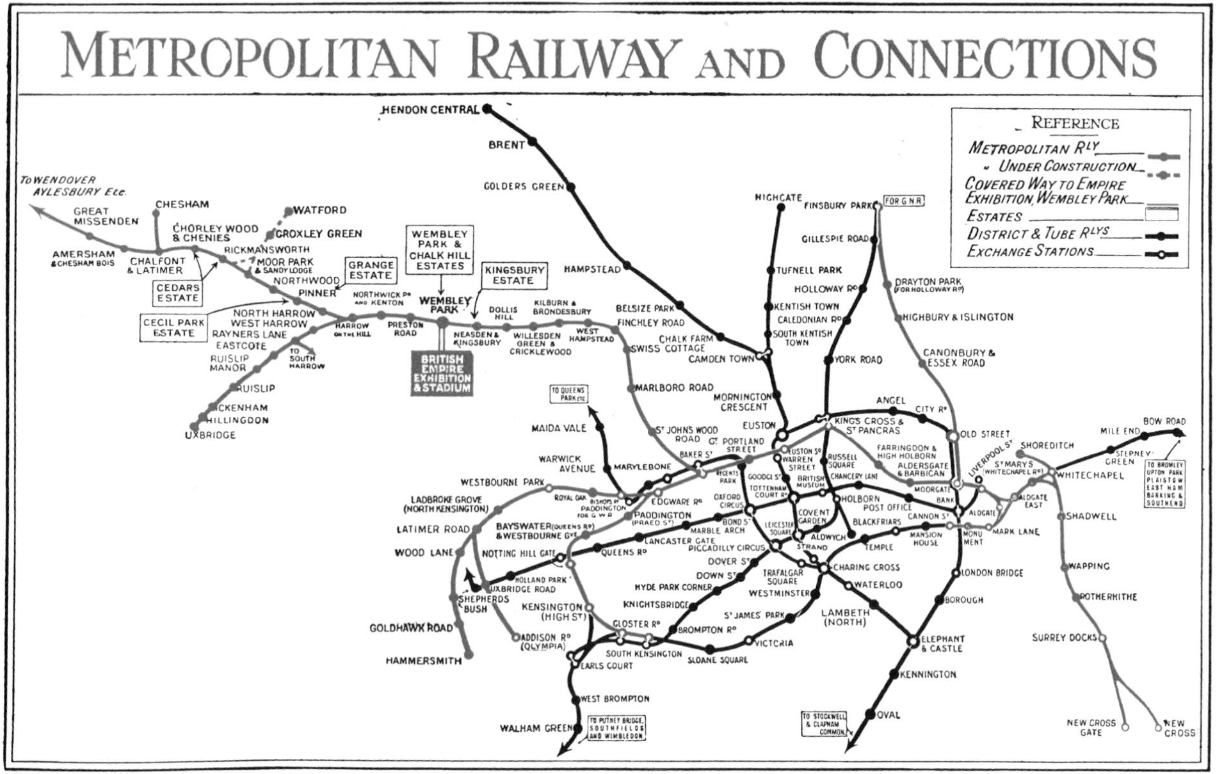
METROPOLITAN RAILWAY AND CONNECTIONS
REFERENCE
METROPOLITAN R^LY
" UNDER CONSTRUCTION
COVERED WAY TO EMPIRE EXHIBITION, WEMBLEY PARK
ESTATES
DISTRICT & TUBE R^LYS
EXCHANGE STATIONS
TO WENDOVER AYLESBURY Etc.
GREAT MISSENDEN
AMERSHAM & CHESHAM BOIS
CHESHAM
CHALFONT & LATIMER
CHORLEY WOOD & CHENIES
CEDARS ESTATE
RICKMANSWORTH
WATFORD
CROXLEY GREEN
MOOR PARK & SANDY LODGE
NORTHWOOD
GRANGE ESTATE
PINNER
CECIL PARK ESTATE
NORTH HARROW
WEST HARROW
RAYNERS LANE
EASTCOTE
RUISLIP MANOR
RUISLIP
ICKENHAM
HILLINGDON
UXBRIDGE
TO SOUTH HARROW
HARROW ON THE HILL
NORTHWICK P^K AND KENTON
PRESTON ROAD
WEMBLEY PARK & CHALK HILL ESTATES
WEMBLEY PARK
BRITISH EMPIRE EXHIBITION & STADIUM
KINGSBURY ESTATE
NEASDEN & KINGSBURY
DOLLIS HILL
WILLESDEN GREEN & CRICKLEWOOD
KILBURN & BRONDESBURY
WEST HAMPSTEAD
FINCHLEY ROAD
SWISS COTTAGE
MARLBORO ROAD
ST JOHNS WOOD ROAD
BAKER ST
HENDON CENTRAL
BRENT
GOLDERS GREEN
HAMPSTEAD
BELSIZE PARK
CHALK FARM
CAMDEN TOWN
MORNINGTON CRESCENT
EUSTON
HIGHGATE
TUFNELL PARK
KENTISH TOWN
SOUTH KENTISH TOWN
FINSBURY PARK
FOR G N R
GILLESPIE ROAD
HOLLOWAY R^D
CALEDONIAN R^D
YORK ROAD
DRAYTON PARK (FOR HOLLOWAY R^D)
HIGHBURY & ISLINGTON
CANONBURY & ESSEX ROAD
ANGEL
CITY R^D
OLD STREET
KINGS CROSS & ST PANCRAS
FARRINGDON & HIGH HOLBORN
ALDERSGATE & BARBICAN
MOORGATE
BANK
LIVERPOOL ST
SHOREDITCH
ST MARYS (WHITECHAPEL R^D)
WHITECHAPEL
STEPNEY GREEN
MILE END
BOW ROAD
TO BROMLEY UPTON PARK PLAISTOW EAST HAM BARKING & SOUTHEND
ALDGATE EAST
ALDGATE
MARK LANE
MONUMENT
SHADWELL
WAPPING
ROTHERHITHE
SURREY DOCKS
NEW CROSS GATE
NEW CROSS
TO QUEENS PARK ETC
MAIDA VALE
WARWICK AVENUE
MARYLEBONE
WESTBOURNE PARK
ROYAL OAK
BISHOPS R^D PADDINGTON FOR G W R
EDGWARE R^D
PADDINGTON (PRAED ST)
LADBROKE GROVE (NORTH KENSINGTON)
LATIMER ROAD
WOOD LANE
SHEPHERDS BUSH
GOLDHAWK ROAD
HAMMERSMITH
BAYSWATER (QUEENS R^D) & WESTBOURNE G^VE
NOTTING HILL GATE
HOLLAND PARK
UXBRIDGE ROAD
QUEENS R^D
LANCASTER GATE
MARBLE ARCH
BOND ST
OXFORD CIRCUS
REGENTS PARK
GT PORTLAND STREET
EUSTON SQ
WARREN STREET
GOODGE ST
TOTTENHAM COURT R^D
BRITISH MUSEUM
RUSSELL SQUARE
CHANCERY LANE
HOLBORN
POST OFFICE
COVENT GARDEN
LEICESTER SQUARE
ALDWYCH
STRAND
PICCADILLY CIRCUS
DOVER ST
DOWN ST
HYDE PARK CORNER
KNIGHTSBRIDGE
BROMPTON R^D
TRAFALGAR SQUARE
CHARING CROSS
WESTMINSTER
ST JAMES' PARK
VICTORIA
SLOANE SQUARE
SOUTH KENSINGTON
GLOSTER R^D
KENSINGTON (HIGH ST)
ADDISON R^D (OLYMPIA)
EARLS COURT
WEST BROMPTON
WALHAM GREEN
TO PUTNEY BRIDGE, SOUTHFIELDS AND WIMBLEDON
BLACKFRIARS
TEMPLE
MANSION HOUSE
CANNON ST
LONDON BRIDGE
BOROUGH
WATERLOO
LAMBETH (NORTH)
ELEPHANT & CASTLE
KENNINGTON
OVAL
TO STOCKWELL & CLAPHAM COMMON

THATCHED COTAGE IN METRO-LAND.

FOREWORD.

THE Metropolitan Railway—the World's Pioneer Underground System—was primarily built to provide convenient means for rapid transit round and across London and ready access to the terminal stations of the various trunk lines.   But the Company also has an important Extension line from Baker Street which runs out into the delightful country situated in Middlesex, Herts and Bucks.

The district through which it passes has been happily named Metroland, and it is the purpose of this Guide briefly to describe the more important of the small townships and villages which the Metropolitan serves, and in the steady development of which the line has been the principal agent.   Metro-land is one of the most beautiful areas in the Home Counties.   Its share

AT QUAINTON ROAD.

of the Buckinghamshire Chilterns is as picturesque and diversified as anything that Kent, Surrey or Sussex has to show.

A special feature of this handbook is the section entitled " Country Homes in Metro-land." This contains full particulars of the various residential districts served by the system, and it also deals with the activities of the Metropolitan Railway Country Estates, Ltd., who are developing certain choice Estates aggregating about 627 acres. The Company has already built numerous houses, both large and small, which can be acquired on payment of an agreed deposit with the balance spread over a period of years as rent. Several other building estate companies are at work on other favoured sites, and contributing their quota, on the most modern lines, to the solution of the housing problem.

The many advantages of ownership must be obvious to every householder. Secure from the tenant's uneasy feeling that his lease is running out and that he may receive notice to quit, the owner has the gratification of knowing that, so long as the

CHALFONT ST. GILES

property belongs to him, all the improvements he may make to the house and garden are for his own benefit and that of his family—not for the Landlord.

As a Holiday Line, the " Metro." enjoys a steadily increasing popularity for Excursions and Pleasure Parties of all kinds. In this respect it offers attractions equal and in some respects superior to any other railway, for it rapidly conducts those who travel by it into secluded rural districts which still retain much of their freshness unspoilt. The roads are good and well adapted for cycling, and for those who walk there are field-paths and wood-paths in rich and varied abundance.

For the latter the Company has issued a series of handy booklets, graphically describing numerous characteristic rambles starting from the various stations served. The detailed descriptions enable anyone to find his way without carrying a map or relying on enquiry, and as the walks have been planned to avoid the high-roads as much as possible, they have already been found of use and pleasure by a very large number of walkers.

PANORAMIC VIEW OF BRITISH EMPIRE EXHIBITION.

10

METRO·LAND

BRITISH
EMPIRE
EXHIBITION
SECTION

ENTRANCE COURTS OF EXHIBITION.

INTRODUCTION.

THE British Empire Exhibition will be the chief event of 1924. Never before has an Exhibition on such an elaborate scale been prepared. It is costing over £10,000,000 to produce, and an entirely new concrete city has been erected to house it. The most conservative expert calculations put the probable number of visitors between April and October at a minimum of 25,000,000. Though its exhibits will be confined to the British Empire, in all but in name the Exhibition will be international, for the British Empire covers a quarter of the known globe, and every one of the Dominions and Colonies within its bounds is taking part.

The grounds at Wembley will reproduce in miniature the entire resources of the British Empire. There you will be able to inspect the Empire from end to end. From Canada it is but a stone's throw to Australia, from Australia a short step to India and the Far East, from Hong Kong a few minutes' walk to New Zealand or Malay. In a single day you will be able to learn more geography than a year of hard study would teach you, and see in each case the conditions of life of the country you are visiting.

Maybe, you have often wanted to travel round the world. At Wembley you will be able to do so at a minimum of cost, in a minimum of time, with a minimum of trouble, studying as you go the shop windows of the British Empire. You will be able to go behind those windows and see how the goods are produced and meet the men and women who produce them. Every aspect of life, civilised and uncivilised, will be shown in an Exhibition which is the last word in comfort and convenience.

BRITISH GOVERNMENT PAVILION.

BRITISH GOVERNMENT PAVILION.

THE British Government is erecting a Pavilion of appropriate dignity of structure and design. The Royal Suite for the use of the King and Queen will overlook the portico, which will be supported by columns thirty-two feet high, and will be guarded by six massive lions, symbolical of the might and dignity of the Empire. The Navy, Army and Air Force are organizing impressive displays, and many important aspects of Empire communication, Empire trade, Empire settlement and Imperial economic development will be presented. On a water stage seventy feet wide, which, by an ingenious mechanical arrangement, can be converted in a few minutes into an ordinary stage for other displays, certain historical episodes on sea and land and in the air will be realistically reproduced. The Air Force exhibition of models will be supplemented by exhibits of actual aeroplanes and aircraft in an aerodrome easily accessible from the Exhibition grounds. In the Central Court of Honour of the Pavilion, a gigantic model relief map of the world will show by changing lights the growth and extent of the Empire, its resources, development and population. The home country's productive capacity in relation to its ability to manufacture goods for export, and the importance of British overseas trade, will also be illustrated by a large scale model of Great Britain and Ireland. In an annexe there will be a cinema theatre where films of Imperial interest will be in continuous display. The Royal Mint, which will show a complete set of coins of the Empire and of British war medals, will strike special commemorative plaques. The Ministry of Health, Ministry of Agriculture and other Departments will also be represented.

PALACE OF INDUSTRY.

PALACE OF INDUSTRY.

THE Palace of Industry, which is only slightly smaller in size than the Palace of Engineering, will house such industries of the United Kingdom as do not come under the general heading of engineering. The largest single exhibit will be that given by the Chemical industry, which in all will occupy an area of 37,500 square feet. The central feature of the display will be an exhibit of research in pure chemistry, in which the Association of British Chemical Manufacturers, which has organized the whole Chemical Section, is being aided by the Royal Society.

Cotton textiles will occupy 32,187 square feet. A representative Committee covering all Lancashire cotton interests is organizing the section. The whole story of cotton production will be illustrated from the growing of the raw material to a complete working range of every kind of cotton textile machinery, ending in groups of exhibits of every sort of finished product. Wool textiles, organized by a powerful Committee at Bradford, will fill 15,000 square feet.

Ulster and her industries will occupy 6,187 square feet. The unique status of the Government of Northern Ireland within the Empire is emphasised at the Exhibition. Instead of having a separate pavilion in the grounds, the Government has taken one of the most prominent corners in the Palace of Industry, and is organizing there a show of the principal Ulster industries, including shipbuilding, flax and linen, and beverages.

In the section devoted to musical instruments the visitor will be able to hear every sort of British instrument in a series of sound-proof rooms.

PALACE OF ENGINEERING.

THE Palace of Engineering is probably the largest concrete building in the world. It covers an area six and a half times the size of Trafalgar Square, and has a floor space of over half a million square feet. Five full-size railway lines, connecting with the main trunk lines of the country, traverse the building from end to end to enable exhibits to be put in place quickly. Five huge overhead cranes serve to swing exhibits from the trucks in which they arrive into positions they are to occupy.

The section devoted to shipbuilding, marine, mechanical and general engineering, will form probably the finest display of general engineering ever brought together in any one exhibition. The electrical engineering section will contain as an exhibit a monster power station, to the making of which forty firms are contributing. This will provide electricity for running all the machinery in the various sections of the Exhibition, and for lighting the entire Exhibition at night.

In the Motor Transport Section will be representative exhibits of motor-cars, motors and accessories. In the Land Transport Section will be found the exhibits of the great railway companies and of the chief makers of rolling stock. In this section the " Metro " have secured considerable space, and are presenting an exhibit of outstanding interest. This exhibit, which should be visited by all, will comprise a latest type electric car; huge relief model map covering districts served by the " Metro "; actual working train control diagram, showing movement of trains; model of typical " Metro-land " residence, and an Information Bureau where full information upon all matters can be obtained.

AUSTRALIAN PAVILION.

AUSTRALIA.

AUSTRALIA'S site covers an area of approximately five-and-a-half acres; her Pavilion is as big as the whole of Olympia. In a gallery at one end there will be an Australian restaurant, where practically all the food-stuffs used will be of Australian production—bread, fruit, butter and meat and where only Australian wines will be served.

The resources of this vast and still largely undeveloped country will be illustrated by actual exhibits. About fifty of the famous Australian Merino Sheep will be exhibited alive in the grounds, and there will be periodic sheep-shearing displays in the Pavilion. The principal sections will be devoted to pastoral industries, dairy products, orchards and gardens, forestry, cereals, fodders and plants, cottons, vineyards, manufactures, mining, shipping and transportation. There will be a cinema theatre capable of seating 500 people, in which will be shown continuously films illustrating life in Australia and the industries of the Commonwealth.

The grounds surrounding the Pavilion will be laid out in gardens with Australian plants and trees. Amongst them will be a large quantity of wonderful tree ferns, which, with their out-spreading fronds, often attain a height of 12 feet. A great cold storage will be shown, together with Australian refrigerated products, such as butter, meat, eggs and poultry. The Commonwealth Bank will have a branch in the building, and a special reading room will provide a wide range of Australian newspapers and general literature relating to the country.

Australia's small neighbour, Fiji, will be represented in a separate Pavilion of her own.

NEW ZEALAND.

NEW ZEALAND'S site covers an area of approximately 132,400 square feet, of which 45,500 square feet are occupied by the Pavilion. Its exterior will be handsomely decorated in fibrous plaster with typical New Zealand scenes. There will be an imposing entrance, leading into the main hall, in which New Zealand natural history exhibits, tourist and sporting trophies, will be displayed. The Pavilion will be divided into sections, in which will be shown the various products and industries of the Dominion. Provision will be made for meat, dairy produce, fruit and fisheries—all in cold storage—and near the fresh fruit exhibit will be preserved fruit and jams. The fisheries section will illustrate the sporting possibilities of the Dominion, and specimens of sword-fish, king fish, and others will be shown in blocks of ice. There will also be exhibits of wool, hides, skins, tallow, rabbit and opossum skins, minerals, seeds, honey, kauri gum, poultry, flax, timber and other secondary industries. A garden of over two acres adjoining the Pavilion will give a representative display of New Zealand plants, foliage and grasses.

A Cinema will be provided, in which films will be shown depicting New Zealand life, industries and scenery, and Maori customs and folklore. At a Restaurant in the Pavilion it will be possible to obtain meals made entirely from New Zealand products.

An interesting feature of the section will be the Carved Maori House (Matatua) in the grounds, which was completed in 1874 on the ratification of peace between two tribes which had been at war for many years.

INDIAN PAVILION.

INDIA.

INDIA'S Pavilion, which covers three acres of ground, will reproduce the artistic beauties of the famous Taj Mahal at Agra and the Jama Masjid at Delhi. It is made of steel and fibrous plaster and is flanked by minarets 110 ft. high. Over the main gateway is an imposing white dome. Before the Pavilion is a sunken courtyard surrounded by a colonnade.

The arts and crafts, metal work, carpets, curtains, carving in wood and ivory for which India has a world-wide reputation, will all be displayed in the Pavilion. There will be models showing the famous Khyber Pass and those parts of the Frontier where the Chitral and Tirah campaigns were fought. Other models will show the advance which has been made in railway construction, and His Royal Highness the Prince of Wales is kindly lending a model of the railway saloon built for him in India, which he used on his recent tour. The activity of India's ports, the best possible index of her commercial prosperity, will be a special feature of the Pavilion. The Empire will thus be informed of the volume of trade that passes through Calcutta, Bombay and Karachi, and will see how the transport problems of the East are solved. Indian timber and its uses will form the subject of a particularly attractive and instructive court, organized by the Indian Forest Department.

Many of the Indian princes have taken space in which the varied resources of their States will be shown on a scale never attempted before. Each State and Province is undertaking the arrangement of its own court. The grounds surrounding the Pavilion will be tastefully laid out. An Indian luncheon and tea-room will be found among the trees to the north.

18

CANADIAN PAVILION.

CANADA.

THE Canadian Pavilion, an imposing building in neo-Grec style, will contain a complete range of the natural and manufactured products of Canada. Agriculture will form one of the outstanding features of the Pavilion, and samples of all agricultural products will be attractively displayed. Mineral specimens, representative of practically every producing mine in the Dominion, will be on view. This will give the visitor an idea of the immense value of Canada's mineral wealth. Specimens of all woods grown in Canada will be shown in the Forestry Section. Horticulture will be represented by a varied display of both fresh and preserved fruits, set out in a typical Canadian orchard, which will illustrate the methods of cultivation used in the West.

Samples of all the leading manufactured goods in the country will be arranged in different parts of the Pavilion, and representatives of individual firms will be in attendance to quote prices and dates of delivery. From this display the Home Country will see what vast strides Canada is making along industrial lines. A special section will be devoted to the educational facilities offered in the Dominion. Suitable reading and rest rooms will be provided.

On each side of the main building will be Pavilions containing exhibits made by the Canadian National Railway and Canadian Pacific Railway. These exhibits will illustrate the wonderful transportation systems which Canada possesses, and will give all possible information as to the many attractions that the Dominion has to offer alike to the tourist, prospective settler and investor.

SOUTH AFRICA.

THE Pavilion of the Union of South Africa, covering an area of 50,000 square feet, will be built in the old Dutch style. The entrances have characteristic Dutch gables, which, with the stoep and loggia, give the building a distinctive South African appearance.

In the grounds on the western side of the building the South African Railways will install a South African train composed of a dining-car, travelling saloon, and a kitchen and staff car. Meals will be served to visitors on the train in order to illustrate the facilities and comfort of travelling on the Union Railways. On the left-hand side of the building an ostrich paddock is being provided, and a number of live birds in full plumage will be shown. Demonstrations will be given at regular intervals, showing the manner in which feathers are cut from the birds. The gardens in front of the Pavilion will be planted with typical South African plants, such as geranium, montbretia, gladiolus and Cape heath.

The principal exhibits will be wool, mohair, ostrich feathers, fruit, wines, dried fruits, canned fruits, minerals, and manufactured goods.

A complete working model of a diamond washing plant will be erected, and arrangements are being made for demonstrations of diamond cutting and polishing. Rhodesia, Tristan da Cunha, Swaziland, and Bechuanaland will be represented by attractive stands in the Pavilion. Cape Town and Durban are arranging special exhibits of harbour facilities.

One cinema will show films of South Africa's industries, and another will depict its travel facilities. scenery and history.

NEWFOUNDLAND PAVILION.

NEWFOUNDLAND.

NEWFOUNDLAND'S Pavilion will contain a complete range of the varied products for which the oldest colony in the British Empire is famous. The mineral resources, forest products and manufactures of the island will all find a place in a handsome building which stands on a site of 27,000 square feet.

Special prominence will be given to displays of the furs and pelts found in the islands. All kinds of fox skins—silver, black, red and white—come from Newfoundland. These, with seal-skins and the skins of ermine, bear, marten, otter, muskrat, lynx, wolf and caribou will all be attractively laid out. Newfoundland sealskin, converted into beautifully finished leather for a variety of industrial and artistic purposes, equals the finest Morocco leather. From Newfoundland also comes the best cod liver oil in the world. Its production will be explained by a series of fishery exhibits.

Iron ore will be brought from the famous Bell Island, near St. John's, one of the largest mines in the world, and the amazing variety of products for which it is used, ranging from railway iron and wire fencing to the most delicate steel for munitions of war, will be illustrated.

An extensive exhibit of forest products will show the importance of the recently developed "newsprint" paper, which is now of the finest quality, and is used widely by newspapers in Great Britain and elsewhere.

An interesting historical display will be given of the relics of the Beothics, the aboriginal people of the island, the last of whom died out over a century ago.

WEST AFRICAN EXHIBIT.

WEST AFRICA, BERMUDA, WEST INDIES, Etc.

THE West African Section takes the form of a walled town, and is an exact replica of a typical city in the hinterland of West Africa. It covers an area of over three acres, and contains three Pavilions, representing Nigeria, the Gold Coast and Sierra Leone. The exact conditions under which the West African people live will be reproduced, and special quarters arranged for some seventy representatives of the Yoruba, Fanti, Hausa and Mendi tribes. Forty thousand feet of film will be on view daily, showing the natural beauties of Nigeria and the Gold Coast.

The West Indian and Atlantic Group, which comprises the Falkland Islands, British Honduras, Barbadoes, Jamaica, Bahamas, Trinidad and Tobago, and the Windward and Leeward Islands, will occupy a Pavilion in the Colonial Georgian style. British Guiana, which will occupy the entire south wing of the West Indies Pavilion, is erecting a fine model of the famous Kaieteur Waterfall, the highest known single drop fall in the world. A full working model of an alluvial gold and diamond pit, operated by native workmen, will be staged.

The East African building covers about 16,250 square feet, and is a copy of an actual Arab building. The entrance door will be a replica of one of the beautiful old carved Arab doorways in Zanzibar. Various courts will be devoted to the attractions of the Sudan, Kenya, Uganda, Tanganyika, Zanzibar, Nyasaland, Mauritius and the Seychelles.

Illustrations of Bermuda will call public attention to its marvellous climate, the infinite variety of its natural beauty, and its sporting attractions.

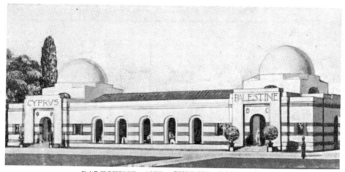

PALESTINE AND CYPRUS PAVILION.

BURMA, PALESTINE, CEYLON, ETC.

BURMA'S Section, which adjoins the Indian grounds, contains a Pavilion designed on purely Burmese lines decorated by some of the finest carving in the Exhibition. For the most part this has been prepared in Burma, and will be sent over ready to be set up. At the main entrance will be a bridge-house copied from one of the gates of the famous Arakan Pagoda at Mandalay.

The Ceylon Pavilion is in the Kandyan style of architecture. The towers flanking it on each side are modelled upon the well-known " Temple of the Tooth " at Kandy, and the panels surrounding the entrance porches are copies of characteristic figures in the Kandyan decoration.

One hundred and seventy-five Chinese will be found at work in the Hong Kong Section, which will take the form of an exact reproduction of a street in Hong Kong, with a Chinese restaurant, shops, and typical native products.

The Malaya Section will display the produce and commerce of the Straits Settlement, the Federated Malay States and the Unfederated States. The Pavilion reproduces the Moorish-Arabesque style of architecture used in the public buildings of Malaya. Sarawak, which is being accommodated on the Malay site, is erecting a pavilion which is to be a replica of the residence of His Highness the Rajah.

The Palestine and Cyprus Pavilion is designed in the style followed in the Eastern Mediterranean. A feature of the building will be a Verandah Café, in which light refreshments and wines will be served. Malta, in a special pavilion, will concentrate upon illustrating its own historical importance.

SECTION OF MODEL COAL MINE.

AMUSEMENTS PARK.

THE Amusements Park at the Exhibition will be on a scale hitherto unknown in this country. It will cover a space of forty-seven acres, where more than a million pounds capital has been invested to provide for the lighter hours of visitors. Beside the larger and more elaborate attractions, the side shows will number fully a thousand.

At one end of the Amusements Park will be a scenic railway and switchback, giving a run of a mile, and at the other end two " Coasters " will race each other for the same distance, their speed depending on the energy of their occupants.

" Dream Land " is the name given to a wonderful children's playground, where kiddies may be left in charge of trained nurses, while parents explore the wonders of other parts. In this children's wonderland the "Old Woman who lived in a Shoe " will be ready to entertain her little guests; she will have see-saws, swings, rocking-horses, miniature railways, and a host of other amusement devices, all of which are a joy to every child.

There will also be an exact replica of a coal-mine, through which 2,000 people will be able to pass per hour.

A magnificent Dancing Hall twice the size of the Albert Hall, will be a great attraction. So will be a unique and wonderful Aquarium stocked with the queerest live fishes from the depths of the farthest oceans. The Temple of Beauty may also be mentioned, where, in the costumes of their respective periods, many of the most famous historical beauties will appear reincarnated in all their loveliness for the period of the Exhibition.

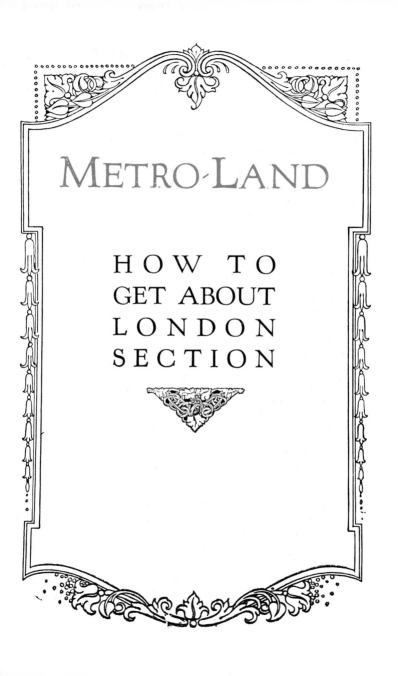

METRO·LAND

HOW TO
GET ABOUT
LONDON
SECTION

FLEET STREET AND LAW COURTS.

ST. PAUL'S CATHEDRAL.

HOW TO GET ABOUT LONDON.

THE visitor will find in the railways of the Metropolis the golden key to easy and inexpensive transport. They radiate to all points of the compass, and form so effective a network as to leave no part of London inaccessible. All these railways are operated by electic power.

There are in the area known as Greater London upwards of 600 passenger railway stations. The length of passenger lines in the same area is 661 miles. The " tube " and other underground railway stations number about 130. One is rarely more than a few hundred yards distant from a station in London proper.

Foremost among these railways stands the Metropolitan Railway—the pioneer Underground system of the world—with a record for density of railway operation which has no equal. The " Metro " goes North, South, East and West; links up at eight points with London's Tube system; provides convenient connection with the termini of the great Trunk railways and also affords speedy and comfortable travel at the minimum of cost.

Although London is so big that it would take months to visit its numberless streets, and years to know intimately the

WESTMINSTER BRIDGE.

details of the suburbs, the features which appeal most strongly to sightseers are, with few exceptions, confined to a central area, lying for the most part north of the Thames, and measuring roughly some five miles from west to east, and three from north to south.

It will greatly assist the stranger in getting about if he forms at the outset a mental picture of the direction and inter-sections of the principal thoroughfares. When he has memorised these the position of the most convenient railway stations can be readily fixed. For that reason, as likely to be more helpful than pages of elaborate directions, key plans have been introduced into this Guide (see pp. 32 and 33), showing the principal thoroughfares in relation to London's historical buildings, museums, theatres and music halls, together with the most convenient stations.

A careful study of these key plans will show how readily accessible are London's places of interest, and visitors who desire to see all the great national memorials, Westminster Abbey, St. Paul's, the Tower, the Mint, the Houses of Parliament, the Inns of Court and so on, will find a " Metro " or other railway station ready at hand to afford rapid transit, free from the confusion and congestion inseparable from the surface of London's streets.

TOWER BRIDGE.

THE " METRO " ROUTE TO THE EXHIBITION.

THE Metropolitan Railway provides the easiest, quickest and best route to the British Empire Exhibition. Its train service is unequalled for frequency and rapidity; it is the most convenient and most comfortable line.

The time-saving merits of the service are also beyond question : for instance, the journey by the fast trains from Baker Street to Wembley Park occupies only 10 minutes; from Euston Square only 14 minutes; King's Cross, 16 minutes; Moorgate, 20 minutes; and from other points in London the journey time is relatively no less rapid.

In addition to large scale rebuilding operations carried out at Wembley Park, which include a covered way direct into the Exhibition Grounds, extensive improvements are also in evidence throughout the Company's system to add to the comfort of those using the line.

A practically continuous service of trains will be maintained to and from Wembley Park this summer, and although all ways will lead to Wembley, the " Metro," with its unrivalled organization and directness of route, will undoubtedly be found to be the best, quickest and most convenient way to the greatest Exhibition ever held in this country.

ROYAL EXCHANGE AND BANK OF ENGLAND.

The new " Metro " Wembley Park Station represents one of the finest and most efficiently equipped stations erected for the handling of large crowds. Its platforms aggregate over 2,500 feet; and a large covered way takes the passenger direct into the Exhibition grounds, under shelter all the way. Actually linked to this covered way is the North End Station of the " Never-stop " railway, a wonderful endless moving track, surmounted by cars, capable of handling 12,000 passengers per hour. This railway connects various parts of the Exhibition, travels between stations at a speed of 24 miles per hour, and automatically slows down in the five stations provided to 2 miles an hour to enable passengers to enter and alight.

Nineteen Booking Windows have been provided at Wembley Park Station to deal expeditiously with return Exhibition traffic.

Special arrangements have been made at Exchange stations to deal with the crowds which will arrive from the North and elsewhere at London's main line termini, and additional booking windows will be opened to obviate delay.

Additional entrances and exits have been made in the main circulating area at Baker St. Station, and a new entrance, with booking office complete, has been provided in Marylebone Road.

MANSION HOUSE AND CHEAPSIDE.

As an aid to the public, a handy pocket folder Map has been prepared which shows at a glance the " Metro " route to the Exhibition, from all parts of London, in addition to other useful information. Copies of this map may be obtained, free, at any " Metro " Booking Office.

On the occasion of the 1923 Cup Tie Final the " Metro " carried, without " hold-up " or mishap, no fewer than 152,000 passengers within a period of four hours. At the peak of the traffic passengers were deposited at Wembley Park Station at the amazing rate of a thousand a minute. They were got away after the match with equal rapidity.

The " Metro " rolling stock available for Exhibition traffic would, if placed end-on, extend a distance of six and a half miles, or in other words, it would form a continuous train stretching from Baker Street to Wembley Park Station. Between Baker Street and Wembley Park no fewer than 338 automatic and power controlled signals have been installed.

Duplicate " Up " and " Down " lines from Finchley Road give the " Metro " the advantage of clear tracks for non-stop trains in both directions, and twenty 60-mile-an-hour electric locomotives will be brought into use to provide the maximum number of express trains.

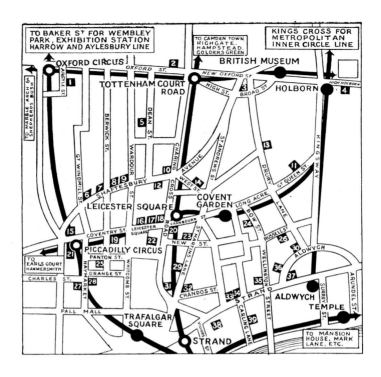

KEY PLAN SHOWING LONDON THEATRES
AND MUSIC HALLS

1. Palladium	14. Ambassadors	27. His Majesty's
2. Oxford	15. Pavilion	28. Haymarket
3. Princes	16. Empire	29. Duke of York's
4. Holborn Empire	17. Daly's	30. Aldwych
5. New Royalty	18. Hippodrome	31. Garrick
6. Lyric	19. Prince of Wales	32. Coliseum
7. Apollo	20. Wyndham's	33. Adelphi
8. Globe	21. Criterion	34. Vaudeville
9. Queen's	22. Alhambra	35. Lyceum
10. Palace	23. New	36. Strand
11. Kingsway	24. Covent Garden	37. Gaiety
12. Shaftesbury	25. Comedy	38. Little
13. Winter Garden	26. Drury Lane	39. Savoy

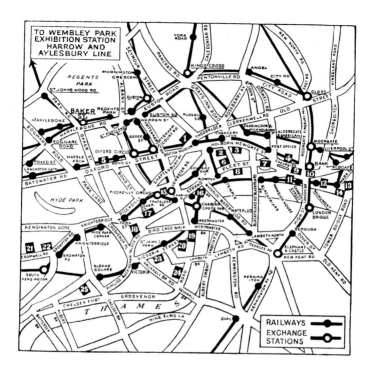

KEY PLAN SHOWING LONDON HISTORICAL
BUILDINGS, MUSEUMS, Etc.

1. British Museum
2. Lincoln's Inn
3. Staple Inn
4. Guildhall
5. Wallace Collection
6. Law Courts
7. St. Paul's Cathedral
8. Temple
9. Bank of England
10. Royal Exchange
11. Mansion House
12. Monument

13. Mint
14. Tower of London
15. National Gallery
16. Cleopatra's Needle
17. St. James' Palace
18. Buckingham Palace
19. Houses of Parliament
20. Westminster Abbey
21. Natural History Museum
22. Victoria & Albert Museum
23. Westminster Cathedral
24. Tate Gallery
25. Chelsea Hospital

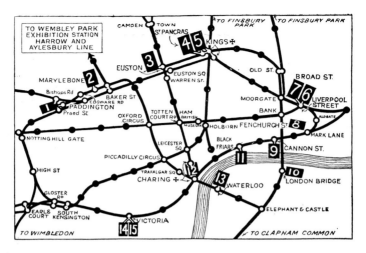

KEY PLAN SHOWING LONDON MAIN LINE
RAILWAY TERMINI WITH CONNECTIONS

No.	Main Line Station	Connecting Station a	Remarks
1	Paddington	Praed Street (Metro.) ... Bishop's Road (Metro.)	Subway Covered way
2	Marylebone	Edgware Road (Metro.) Baker Street (Metro.) ...	3 min. walk 5 min. walk
3	Euston	Euston Square (Metro.)	5 min. walk
4	St. Pancras	King's Cross (Metro.) ...	1 min. walk
5	King's Cross	King's Cross (Metro.) ...	Subway
6	Liverpool Street	Liverpool Street (Metro.)	Subway
7	Broad Street	Liverpool Street (Metro.)	Adjoins
8	Fenchurch Street... ...	Mark Lane (Metro. and District) Aldgate (Metro.) ...	3 min. walk 5 min. walk
9	Cannon Street	Cannon Street (Metro. and District)	Subway
10	London Bridge	Monument (Metro. and District)	5 min. walk
11	St. Paul's	Blackfriars (District) ...	Covered way
12	Charing Cross	Charing Cross (District) Trafalgar Square (Bak'rloo)	Short walk Short walk
13	Waterloo	Waterloo (Bakerloo) ...	Covered way
14 15	Victoria ... ... Victoria	} Victoria (District) ...	Subways

34

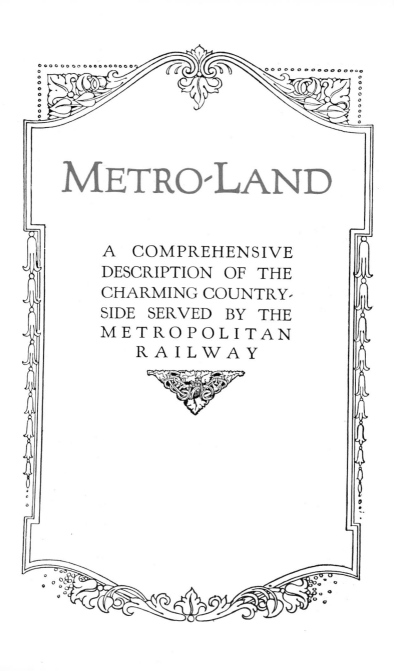

METRO·LAND

A COMPREHENSIVE
DESCRIPTION OF THE
CHARMING COUNTRY-
SIDE SERVED BY THE
METROPOLITAN
RAILWAY

AT WEMBLEY PARK.

WEMBLEY PARK.
Baker Street - - - 6½ Miles.

WEMBLEY PARK, as distinct from Wembley proper, distant a mile away on the Harrow Road, will be known to millions of visitors this year from all over the world as the site of the British Empire Exhibition. The Exhibition will be the largest ever held in this country, and will be opened in April. Its many handsome and spacious pavilions will display to the fullest extent the industries, the natural resources and the scientific attainments of Great Britain, the Dominions Overseas, and many of the more important Crown Colonies. The Exhibition will also include a magnificent Amusements Park.

Within the grounds of the Exhibition, which cover 215 acres, is a vast National Sports Ground, with seats for 30,000 spectators, and room for a hundred thousand others. The

AT WEMBLEY PARK.

AT ICKENHAM.

AT WEMBLEY PARK

Final of the English Cup and the principal meetings of the Amateur Athletic Association are held in its splendid arena.

Wembley Park has been rapidly developed of recent years as a residential district; the Chalk Hill Estate on the north side of the line having about 100 acres for development, and the Wembley Park Estate to the south of the line having rather less. There is a good golf course on the slopes of Uxendon Hill, and two or three others within a few minutes' journey.

It may be noted that the Empire Exhibition stands in the grounds of an older pleasure park, and that on the summit of the highest ground within it stood the Watkin Tower, which, though it never rose beyond the first stage, was originally planned to overtop the Eiffel Tower by 175 feet. It was demolished about fifteen years ago.

Previous to that the original Wembley Park belonged to the Page family. The estate fell into Chancery, and the " Page millions " still await a successful claimant.

AT WEMBLEY PARK.

AT PRESTON ROAD.

PRESTON ROAD.

Baker Street - - - *7½ Miles.*

PRESTON ROAD is still a wayside halt. Its day will come, but at present only a few houses have been built along the lane which leads up to the hamlet of Preston.

The halt is thus principally used by those who visit the Harrow Golf Club, whose Club House adjoins the Station, and in the summer by the members of the various sports clubs of several large business houses in London which have their grounds in the fields near by.

Preston itself is noted as being the birthplace of John Lyon, the Middlesex yeoman, who founded the famous School at Harrow-on-the-Hill, the spire of whose church is the most prominent feature of the landscape. Part of Lyon's house still remains.

At the farmhouse of Uxendon, to the south-east of Preston, Anthony Babington, who plotted to murder Queen Elizabeth and place Mary, Queen of Scots, on the throne of England, was arrested. It is now a shooting school.

The country between Preston and Kenton on the north side of the railway is singularly untouched by the near presence of London, and there are wide spaces of attractive open country in the direction of Stanmore and Edgware.

AT NORTHWICK PARK.

NORTHWICK PARK & KENTON.
Baker Street - - - *8½ Miles.*

NORTHWICK PARK Station was opened in 1923 to serve the needs of a new residential suburb which has sprung up since the war midway between Preston Road and the eastern slopes of Harrow Hill.

The Northwick Estate derives its name from the title of the lords of the manor—the first Lord Northwick having been ennobled in 1797. The family name was Rushout, and the manor, which was the principal one at Harrow, belonged originally to the Archbishop of Canterbury. The estate is now owned by Capt. Spencer Churchill.

The estate, which includes the very attractive old farmhouse on Woodcock Hill, and a considerable tract of land adjoining Ducker, the Harrow School bathing place, is being laid out with exceptional care.

The houses are generously treated in respect of garden space, and in addition to the Northwick Park Golf Club, which forms part of the estate, a recreation ground of five acres, to be known as the Palæstra, is being provided for tennis, etc., with an attractive pavilion or club house. The course of the Harrow Golf Club adjoins the property on the south side.

AT HARROW.

HARROW-ON-THE-HILL.

Baker Street - - - *9½ Miles.*

THERE are two Harrows. One is the Harrow of the Plain, which of late years has grown very fast, northward towards Wealdstone and the high ground of Harrow Weald, and westward and southward towards Pinner and Roxeth. The latter districts are served by halts. The other Harrow is Harrow-on-the-Hill, crowned nobly by the church and the buildings of the famous school, with a high road along the windy ridge which still retains many traces of its village days.

The School dates from Queen Elizabeth's days, when the warm red brick School House, which is the only building of any antiquity connected with it, was built. Now the hill crest has a fine School Chapel, Library and Memorial Hall. The cricket fields lie on the lower slopes of the hill towards Roxeth, and the pleasant slopes looking towards London were purchased

HARROW SCHOOLS.

AT HARROW.

by subscription among friends of the school to save them from the advancing tide of bricks and mortar.

Harrow Church, " the visible church," whose needle-spire is traced against the sky from ten surrounding counties, was consecrated by Archbishop Anselm in 1094. Some portions of the original Norman structure still remain. There are several brasses, including that of John Lyon, and other monuments of interest. The view from the churchyard is famous.

The residential advantages of Harrow are specially enhanced by the admirable train services. The electric trains are rarely at rest, and by the frequent fast trains Baker Street can be reached in fourteen minutes, and the City, without change, in under half an hour.

At Harrow the electric line to Uxbridge branches off. The first halt is at West Harrow, where a considerable suburb has sprung up, and the next at Rayner's Lane, which still awaits development.

AT HARROW.

HAYDON HALL, EASTCOTE.

AT EASTCOTE.

EASTCOTE.

Baker Street   -   -   -   12¼ Miles.

EASTCOTE is one of the most charming villages in the whole of Middlesex. Many who know it best would probably say that it has no rival and well deserves the title of " the loveliest village of the plain."

The broad plain from the station towards Northolt is indeed of little interest, but the hamlet of Eastcote lies on the other side of the railway along the high road which borders the Pin rivulet and the delightful lanes which run up towards the gentle eminence of Haste Hill, in the direction of Northwood.

There are some houses of age and distinction here, notably Eastcote Hall and Haydon Hall, standing in their own grounds, but the real charm of the place consists in the old farm houses, with their red-tiled barns, a few half-timbered dwellings and a number of picturesque cottages, with gardens where the flowers grow in gay profusion.

Haydon Hall was the family home of the Hawtreys, the most celebrated of whom was Lady Banckes, who defended Corfe Castle for the King against the Parliament in 1643. Her memorial is in Ruislip Church.

Near the station are several sports grounds, and boating may be had on the neighbouring lake, which was made by the Grand Junction Canal Company to provide a feeder for the canal. It still serves that useful purpose. It is about 80 acres in extent, and noted for its large tench and pike.

A little further on is the halt which serves the Ruislip Manor Estate, now being laid out as a Garden City. Other building companies are also busy in the neighbourhood.

RUISLIP COMMON.

RUISLIP.

Baker Street - - - *13¼ Miles.*

RUISLIP is an ancient place, and the parish was the second largest in Middlesex. Its church (St. Martin) has a square tower, and was thoroughly restored half a century ago by Sir Gilbert Scott, when the galleries were removed. It has good windows, and in the chancel several interesting monuments of the Hawtrey family. The remains of some fifteenth century mural paintings may be seen on the walls. The best shows an angel weighing a soul in the balance. A carved oak bread cupboard, which holds the small loaves distributed every Sunday in accordance with a bequest dating from 1697, is also a feature of interest. There are memorials, too, of the Great War in the tablets to the Flying Officers who lost their lives at the neighbouring air camps.

In the old days there was a small Priory at Ruislip

RUISLIP CHURCH

46

AT RUISLIP.

dependent originally on the Abbey of Bec, in Normandy, and then transferred to the Priory of Okeburn, in Wiltshire. The manor passed to the Dean and Canons of Windsor, who are still the owners.

Ruislip Park, on the east side of the main street, has been covered with pleasant villa houses, and the little township is growing rapidly in all directions. Between Ruislip and the next village of Ickenham, past what was once the hamlet of Kingsend, are large depôts of the Royal Air Force which have quite altered the character of a district which till the war was of a purely agricultural character.

Ruislip has several tea-gardens, some with recreation grounds attached, which are popular places of resort in the summer time. On the north side of Ruislip, beyond the hamlet of Bury-street, the ground rises to Duck's Hill and Copse Wood, and the whole district towards Harefield and Northwood is most attractive.

NEAR RUISLIP.

AT ICKENHAM.

ICKENHAM.

Baker Street   -   -   -   14½ Miles.

ICKENHAM, despite the neighbouring depôts of the Royal Air Force, still retains at the centre its old-world charm and there are few more typically English villages than this, with its wide open space at the cross-roads, its pond, its inn, its attractive little church, and its suggestion of a big house beyond the tall trees.

The church (St. Giles) has a wooden belfry and tiny spire, and contains several brasses and memorials of the various owners of Swakeleys, a fine Jacobean mansion with ornamental gables and chimney stacks, standing in a park of 300 acres, which is now being laid out as a residential estate. The name of Swakeleys is apparently derived from Swalclyve, who owned the manor in the 14th century. Pepys was a frequent visitor when Sir Robert Vyner lived at the hall in the reign of Charles II. The brook Pin runs through the estate, and has been persuaded with much ingenuity to serve all the purposes of an ornamental lake.

The mound in the churchyard adjoining the road is said to be a fragment of a branch of Grimm's Dyke, which once stretched from Harrow Weald to Uxbridge. Another portion is visible at Eastcote.

AT LATIMER.

NEAR HILLINGDON.

HILLINGDON.

Baker Street - - - *15 Miles.*

ONE of the newest stations opened on the Metropolitan is that at Hillingdon, which is designed to serve part of the new Swakeleys Estate on the " up " side and the new Hillingdon Estate on the " down."

Hillingdon village proper lies some little distance away on the main road from London to Uxbridge. The new Hillingdon is rising on ground which till recently belonged to the parkland of Hillingdon Court.

This was the estate of Lord Hillingdon, whose family name was Mills, of the great banking firm of Glyn, Mills & Co. Hillingdon House adjoining, was built by the last Duke of Schomberg in 1717, and passed through several other distinguished hands, including those of the Chetwynds and the Rockinghams, before it came into the possession of the Cox family.

The flying men took possession of Hillingdon House and its grounds during the war, which are now the Headquarters of the Royal Air Force, Inland Area.

The country adjoining Hillingdon Station has no superior in the neighbourhood for quiet beauty, and the popularity of the new suburb is already well assured.

RIVER FRAYS, UXBRIDGE,

AT UXBRIDGE.

UXBRIDGE.

Baker Street - - - *16¼ Miles.*

THE " Town of Rivers," as Uxbridge might be termed, was well established in times as early as those of King Alfred the Great. At the present day it is the terminal station of the Metropolitan Electric line from Harrow and looks out upon a rich plain, through which flows a medley of small rivers, very difficult to disentangle one from the other. The Grand Junction Canal passes through the outskirts of the town, and in the neighbourhood there are the Pin Brook, which straggles down from Pinner, through Eastcote and Ickenham, and the larger Misbourne, which flows down through Amersham, Chalfont St. Giles and Denham to its confluence with the Colne. Uxbridge thus well deserves its name as the water bridge. There are many bridges and many waters.

In 1645, Commissioners from Charles the First and the Parliament met at Uxbridge in the hope of arriving at terms of settlement. But the attempt was premature and failed. The house where they met has long been known as the " Treaty House," and the room in which the deliberations took place, with its original panelling, is still extant. In the old coaching days Uxbridge was the first " stage " from London on the road to High Wycombe. The coaching inns, very much in their original condition, still adorn the main street.

The industries of Uxbridge consist mainly of flour milling, and the manufacture of iron barrels. There has been considerable residential extension, and there will be still more; for the country around, especially towards that exquisite village, Denham, is among the most beautiful in Middlesex.

AT PINNER.

PINNER.

Baker Street - - - *11¼ Miles.*

UNTIL the coming of the Metropolitan Railway, Pinner was just a sleepy little village, living a secluded life of its own, and devoted to agricultural pursuits. Wheat of particularly excellent quality used to be grown in the neighbourhood, and in the Victorian days there was a large stud farm here which supplied London with many of its best carriage horses and the Shires with some of their best hunters. The railway brought the village into close touch with London, and Pinner began to grow with great rapidity.

It is still spreading fast in all directions, towards Harrow, towards Hatch End, and towards Eastcote. In a retired lane by Nower Hill there are some interesting old houses.

The most picturesque feature of the little town is the High Street, containing several half-timbered and gabled houses and

AT PINNER.

AT PINNER.

cottages and an old inn, which is dated by its gaudy signboard of Queen Anne. The High Street broadens at the top where stands the parish church, a flint building, dating in part from the thirteenth century. It has a good perpendicular tower.

The woodman's axe has been ruthlessly swung among the grand elms, which are still a beautiful feature of Pinner's environment; those who lay out building estates ought to spare every tree they possibly can. The chief feature of interest in the neighbourhood is the ancient moated Headstone Farm, lying between Pinner and Harrow. This was a manor in the possession of the Archbishops of Canterbury, and tradition says that Becket visited it not long before his murder. The moat is still intact and supplied with running water.

The poet Pye, Poet-Laureate before Southey, in George III.'s reign, lived at Pinner, and has a memorial in the church, and Lytton wrote "Eugene Aram" in a gabled cottage at Pinner Wood.

NEAR PINNER

AT NORTHWOOD.

NORTHWOOD.

Baker Street   -   -   -   14 Miles.

IN contrast with many townships on the Metropolitan Extension line, there is little that is ancient about Northwood except perhaps the name of the original hamlet. It is the railway that has made Northwood—a modern suburb in a beautiful country setting.

There are practically two Northwoods, and the Northwood which is the more conspicuous from the railway is not the one which has made Northwood celebrated. This was laid out apparently with the object of setting down as many small houses as possible of the same pattern on an acre of ground, with little regard for the preservation of the old amenities. But the other Northwood, which is not so well seen from the train, is a place of charming villas, large and small, extending on the south side of the line towards the hill which rises to Batchworth Heath, and on the north side up the hill towards Eastbury. Northwood is one of the most popular of the London suburbs on this side, and its population is only limited by the number of houses available. It is twenty-eight minutes distant from Baker Street by the fast trains.

There is much high ground about Northwood. From

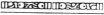

AT NORTHWOOD.

the top of Haste Hill (312 ft.) one of the most pleasing panoramas near London is disclosed. On the high ground on the north of the line in the direction of Watford the Oxhey Woods retain their ancient charm.

Northwood Church is at the foot of the hill leading towards Rickmansworth. It is of flint, with a red-tiled roof and small slate steeple, and dates from 1854, when a new parish was formed out of the parish of Ruislip, taking in parts of the parishes of Watford and Rickmansworth. The most interesting church in the neighbourhood is at Harefield (3 miles to the west). It is full of beautiful monuments of the 17th, 18th and 19th centuries.

A new and particularly pleasing suburb of Northwood is being laid out on the rising ground which leads by Copse Wood on the road to Ruislip. Here contact will be established with the Ruislip Manor Garden City.

The Northwood Golf Club is the oldest on the Metropolitan line, and still maintains its deservedly high reputation and popularity. It extends over many acres towards Poor's Field and the Reservoir.

A feature of Northwood, common to most of the residential districts on the Metropolitan country lines, is the complete absence of factory chimneys.

AT SANDY LODGE

MOOR PARK.

MOOR PARK & SANDY LODGE.

Baker Street - - - *15 Miles.*

THE original halt at Sandy Lodge was opened a few years ago for the accommodation of the Sandy Lodge Golf Club, whose course extends on the north side of the line to the picturesque paper mills on the Colne. It is the driest winter course on this side of London.

Now other golf courses have been laid out in the spacious park of Moor Park on the other side of the railway, and the first beginnings are visible of what cannot fail to be one of London's most beautiful residential districts.

Moor Park itself has a long history, and is associated with many famous names, including Cardinal Wolsey and the Duke of Monmouth. The present mansion house, now the head-quarters of the Golf Club, was designed by Inigo Jones, and its marble hall was built by its then owner out of the spoils of the South Sea Bubble. Its most recent occupants were the first and second Lord Ebury, and on the death of the late owner the whole estate was purchased by Lord Leverhulme for purposes of development. Three golf courses have been laid out in the beautiful undulating grounds.

Batchworth Heath at the top of the hill between Northwood and Rickmansworth is the most picturesque of its kind in the district. Here are one of the entrances to Moor Park, an inn and cricket pitch on the open green, and a fine Georgian house once the residence of Sir Robert Morier, a famous Victorian diplomatist, who is buried in Northwood Churchyard under an enormous recumbent cross of Siberian jasper, the gift of the Tsar Alexander.

TROUT FARM, RICKMANSWORTH.

RICKMANSWORTH.

Baker Street - - - *17½ Miles.*

RICKMANSWORTH, an ancient township of narrow streets, lies most picturesquely in its valley, where a great tongue of Hertfordshire thrusts itself down between Middlesex and Bucks. The Chess, the Gade and the Colne, three pretty streams, here meet and mingle, and supply the Grand Junction Canal, which passes through the outskirts of the town and still carries considerable traffic. The canal bank is well worth following in both directions from Rickmansworth, especially where it makes its way through the picturesque Cassiobury Park, at Watford.

The church of St. Mary's has a long nave with battlemented roof and low windows, good tower and stumpy spire. It contains some memorials of the earlier owners of Moor Park. Its most challenging feature within is the vivid glass in its large east window. A small Roman Catholic Church has been built of recent years at the side of one of the entrances to Rickmansworth Park on the road to Croxley Green.

William Penn, the Quaker, brought his bride, Gulielma Springett, to live at Basing House, in Rickmansworth, and lived there for about five years, before he removed to Sussex.

Moor Park comes down to the confines of the town at

AT RICKMANSWORTH.

Batchworth on the canal; one the other side is Rickmansworth Park, much smaller and with a mansion house of less distinction, but with no less delightful grounds. The edges of the Park are already being appropriated; the eventual fate of the whole estate is no less certain.

On the other side of the road to Chorley Wood a large broad tract of open hillside, named Cedars Estate, is being laid out by the Metropolitan Railway Country Estates Company, which extends from close above the station to the near approaches of Chorley Wood. This is a high-class estate for good houses with generous gardens, and many fine sites are still available.

Visitors to Rickmansworth are now privileged, thanks to the public spirit of Mr. Wilson Young, the owner of Chesswater House (formerly Glen Chess) to see the beautiful grounds of his residence on Wednesdays and Thursdays, between 3.30 and 6 p.m. The Chess flows through the grounds and adds greatly to the beauty of a very skilful example of the landscape-gardener's art. Admission is obtained by gate on the right of the main entrance to the house, which stands in the valley at the foot of Loudwater Lane (indicated by signpost) which turns down to the right out of the Chorley Wood Road, and forms the boundary of Rickmansworth Park. It is hoped that the direction notices in the grounds will be scrupulously observed.

AT CHENIES.

CHORLEY WOOD AND CHENIES
Baker Street - - - *19½ Miles.*

BEAUTIFUL woods, a glorious open common, and a salubrious atmosphere, have attracted many new comers to the favoured locality of Chorley Wood and Chenies, which stands at what may be called the gateway of the Chiltern Hills.

Chenies, a couple of miles or so distant from the railway station, is a beautifully-situated model village, with cottages set at the sides of a triangular green. The village itself is of modern design, and the main charm of Chenies lies in the ancient manor house of the Cheynes—from which it takes its name—which passed some century ago into the possession of the Russells, and in the flint church at its side, set in the beech woods high above the valley of the Chess.

The church contains a mausoleum of the Russells, built by

AT CHENIES.
62

AT CHORLEY WOOD.

the Countess of Bedford in 1556, and still used as a family burial place by the Dukes of Bedford. Many of the monuments are of great beauty. The old name of Chenies was Isenhampstead.

The valley of the Chess, below Chenies on the one side, and the mansion and hamlet of Latimer on the opposite bank, is here at its fairest. The walk from the church through the woods above the river to Chalfont and Latimer Station is extremely attractive. There is a fine stretch of unspoilt and untouched country towards Sarratt and Chipperfield.

Chorley Wood Common which skirts the Metropolitan Railway, is a wide stretch of green elastic turf, diversified with gorse, furze and bracken, over which there is generally a breeze blowing. A Golf Club is established here.

The high plateau on the other side of the line towards Newlands Park is no less beautiful of its kind, and here the beech woods of Bucks may be said to begin. The Hertfordshire boundary line is marked by a pleasant footpath.

CHORLEY WOOD COMMON.

NEAR LATIMER.

CHALFONT AND LATIMER.

Baker Street - - - *21¾ Miles.*

THERE are two Chalfonts :—Chalfont St. Giles and Chalfont St. Peter, twin Buckinghamshire villages on the little river Misbourne, a short two miles apart.

The Chalfonts lie distant three and four miles respectively from the Metropolitan Railway Station in a district which for centuries has been noted for its grand elms, and its profusion of beech and cherry trees. Chalfont St. Giles is associated with John Milton, who in the time of the Great Plague lived in a cottage here, in which he wrote, or rather dictated, the concluding portion of " Paradise Regained." A citizen of the United States some years ago wished to buy the cottage, pull it down, and take it to America for re-erection. It was thereupon placed under trust, and is now, combined with a small library and museum, open to the public. Ellwood, who hired the place for Milton, called it " a pretty box," and so it remains to this day. It was used as an inn in the 18th century and down to 1844 had a porch with a room above it.

The church at Chalfont St. Giles is well situated and contains some striking memorials. It contains a nave and two aisles, and has some 15th and 16th century brasses.

The twin village, Chalfont St. Peter, is hardly so picturesque

AT LATIMER,

as its neighbour, and its brick church is much more plain and
severe. Near by is Jordans, in the burying ground of which
lies William Penn, the founder of Pennsylvania. The tiny
Meeting House, austerely plain, is still in use.

In the close neighbourhood of the Chalfonts are the attractive
estate of Newlands, traversed by many footpaths, and with one
of the rare avenues of old firs in the county; the hamlets of
Horn Hill, on the ridge above the valley of the Colne, and
Seer Green in the direction of Beaconsfield, and several
charming woods. Newlands takes its name from Abraham
Newland, chief cashier of the Bank of England about 1800.

The golf course of Harewood Downs, backed by Pollards,
Wood, on the slopes above the Misbourne Valley, is served
from Chalfont and Latimer Station.

Latimer, the estate of Lord Chesham, formerly tenanted by
Viscount Peel, has a mansion house standing in a perfect position
on rising ground above the Chess and flanked by trim and shapely
woods. It has a small church adjoining, and the little village
is of the " model " order, like that of Chenies. Charles II. is
said to have taken shelter at Latimer in his flight from Worcester
Field.

The lower road towards Flaunden, and the high ridge road
towards Leyhill show the district at its best.

65

NEAR CHESHAM.

NEAR CHESHAM.

CHESHAM.

Baker Street - - - *25¾ Miles.*

CHESHAM, a quiet, but thriving little country town of some 8,000 inhabitants, is served by a branch of the Metropolitan Railway from the main line at Chalfont and Latimer. It is a picturesque blend of old and new, and many gabled houses survive in its narrow streets. It is also a busy place of manufacture as well as a rural market town. In the production of boots, though it cannot vie with Northampton or Leicester, Chesham maintains a sturdy trade of its own. Flour milling, wood-working, chiefly in beech, and, of late, printing, are other industries which give local employment.

The parish church, a fine old flint structure, with tower and spire, stands well in a good situation at the side of a picturesque brick mansion, retired from the main street and approached from one side by a pleasant avenue of trees.

The country round Chesham is split up into shallow valleys, and some of the roads run along the tops of the intervening ridges, spread out like the fingers on a hand. Cholesbury, on its open and breezy common, is one of the pleasantest of the many villages in the neighbourhood. But there are numerous others, such as Hawridge, Chartridge, Leyhill Common and Ashley Green, on the road to Berkhampstead. The beech woods around Chesham are among the finest in the country.

The little river, Chess, has its head springs on the high ground in the direction of Great Missenden, and adds greatly to the attractiveness of the valley. It bears abundant beds of watercress, which is sent away in large quantities to all parts of England, and the spotless white ducks which haunt its waters are as celebrated as those of Aylesbury.

HIGH STREET, AMERSHAM.

AMERSHAM AND CHESHAM BOIS.

Baker Street - - - *23¾ Miles.*

AMERSHAM—a merciful modern corruption of the Saxon Agmondesham—is an ancient county town, which for many centuries enjoyed the distinction of sending a member to Parliament. It was a typical pocket borough during the seventeenth and eighteenth centuries, and the pocket in which it chiefly reposed was that of the reigning lord of the manor—Drake of Shardeloes. It was disfranchised by the Reform Act of 1832.

The old town in the valley of the Misbourne is composed of one long street, of generous width and splendid proportions, with a single branch street in the centre which forms the road to Wycombe. It contains some fine old inns and courtyards, some substantial Georgian houses and gabled cottages and dwellings of an earlier period. The brick town hall—it was town hall above and open market place below, though this is now disused—was the gift of one of the Drakes, and another member of the same family founded the six beautiful little almshouses, also in the main street, built round a tiny court.

The church in the centre of the town contains many good brasses, and several monuments of the Drake family. There is a tradition that John Knox once preached there, and Richard

THE CLUB HOUSE, MOOR PARK.

AMERSHAM.

Baxter disputed within its walls with some Anabaptist soldiers.

The Friends have a pretty little meeting house and burial place in the town on the road to Wycombe, and the whole district is full not only of Quaker but also of much earlier Lollard associations. Amersham, like Chesham, has its local martyrs.

The old seventeenth-century grammar school, formerly in the main street, has been moved up to the new Amersham which has arisen—and is still rising—on the level plateau round the station. It is a flourishing school conducted on the co-education principle of boys and girls being taught in the same classes, and is of course a great boon to the neighbourhood. This new Amersham, in which may be included Amersham Common, is developing at a rapid rate, and many excellent residences have been built round and near the beautiful open common on the road to Chesham Bois. Chesham Bois itself was, centuries ago, one of the residences of the powerful Cheyne family, but the mansion has been gone for two hundred years.

Shardeloes Hall, half a mile from Amersham on the high road to Missenden, is a fine Georgian mansion built near the site of a still earlier house. It is set in glorious woods, and is the home of the Drakes. The spacious lake is a great resort of many species of wild fowl.

NEAR GREAT MISSENDEN.

GREAT MISSENDEN.

Baker Street - - - *29 Miles.*

LELAND, the itinerant topographer of Henry VIII.'s day, writing of Great Missenden, described it as " a praty thoroughfare, but no market town." So it is still.

The pleasant little township, in true Bucks fashion, lies strung out along the main road to Aylesbury, in a typically narrow valley of the Chilterns, which rise steeply on either side the road and line. It is plentifully supplied with old inns and half-timbered, gabled buildings, and thus retains its ancient look.

Here stood a small Priory of Black Canons, founded in 1133, of which no traces remain except such as are included in the buildings of the Hall, which now stands on its site. The parish church clings crouching to the hillside above, and is well worth visiting, though much restored, for its brasses and the unique—so far as the writer knows—Jacobean adornment to the parson's monument on the south wall, *viz.*, a frame of books, which look like bricks.

Great Missenden is developing fast on the Prestwood and Kingswood side; the process has hardly begun on the other side of the valley, where the road climbs up the hill towards picturesque Hyde Heath and Chesham in the one direction and

COTTAGE AT PRESTWOOD.

Ballinger and Lee in the other.

Three miles from Missenden is Great Hampden, home of John Hampden, the Puritan patriot, and one of the ringleaders of the Parliamentary revolt against Charles I. As Disraeli once said, speaking at Hughendon, only a few miles away, " The Revolution was cradled in those hills." Hampden was mortally wounded in a skirmish at Chalgrove, near Thame, and rode slowly home to Great Hampden to die. Hampden House, set in the midst of fine beech woods, is now the seat of the Earl of Buckinghamshire. The common near by is by far the most beautiful in the district. Little Hampden is a mere hamlet in the woods, with a tiny church in a secluded position, which dates from 1254. Its wooden porch with belfry above is its most interesting feature.

Little Missenden, between Great Missenden and Amersham, retains its old character quite untouched by time. No new houses seem to have been built there within living memory, and it lies just off the main road in a quiet backwater of its own. The church possesses an old Norman font. In the Manor House adjoining lived Dr. Bates, a member of the once notorious Hell Fire Club, which included John Wilkes, Whitehead and other Buckinghamshire celebrities. He died at the great age of 98.

AT WENDOVER.

AT WENDOVER.

WENDOVER.

Baker Street - - - *33½ Miles.*

WENDOVER is the pearl of the Chilterns. Its setting is perfect. It lies at the mouth of the break in the hills where the road debouches into the broad Vale of Aylesbury, and the shapely wood-crowned Boddington Hill faces over against the smooth down-like slopes of Coombe Hill, which stands up above the plain like an escarpment. The main street of Wendover itself is almost untouched and quite unspoilt, and gains beauty by its gentle slope, the generous width of its thoroughfare, the charm of its old houses and its pleasing irregularity of plan. There is a new Wendover, but as at Amersham, the new does not jostle and hustle the old. The church, in a lovely setting, lies a quarter of a mile away from the main street at the side of a beautiful old manor house. Here in pre-Reformation days was a famous Rood, and a great resort of pilgrims from the counties round about.

Wendover for several centuries sent a member to the House of Commons, and, like Amersham, was during part of the eighteenth century a close pocket-borough in the possession of the magnificent Earl Verney who ruined the fortunes of his family. On its roll of M.P.'s appear the names of John Hampden, Richard Grenville, " Dick " Steele, Edmund Burke and George Canning—a wonderful galaxy of talent.

The neighbourhood is particularly rich in British camps, owing to the commanding position of the hills near by. During the war the late Mr. Alfred de Rothchild's estate of Halton was transformed into a vast camp of hutments, which played sad havoc with the beauty of the hillside towards Tring, and this has

AT WENDOVER.

developed into one of the principal permanent depôts of the Royal Air Force. The monument on the crest of Coombe Hill is to the memory of the Bucks men who fell in the Boer War.

One branch of the ancient British trackway, the Icknield Way, passes through Wendover from east to west on the lower slopes of the Chilterns. Beyond Coombe Hill it goes through the picturesque villages of Ellesborough and the Kimbles on the way to the Risboroughs. Kimble is the same word as Cymbeline, or Cunobelin, and this is the district associated with the British king of that name.

Chequers, in the gap where the road from Missenden enters the plain, is the historical mansion house and park which the munificence of Lord and Lady Lee of Fareham presented to the nation as a country house for the Prime Ministers of Great Britain. The house was splendidly restored to its original state, and contains many historical relics of Cromwell, one of whose daughters married the then owner of the estate. The beech woods and box-clad ravines in Chequers Park are among the loveliest of their kind. At Welwick House, close to Wendover, there is a tradition that Judge Jeffreys once lived.

From Wendover any number of delightful walking excursions may be made on either side of the line, in the plain or on the hills.

AT AYLESBURY.

AYLESBURY.

Baker Street - - - *38¼ Miles.*

AYLESBURY is the county town of Bucks, a town of assize of great antiquity, beautifully situated on gently rising ground in the rich vale to which it gives its name. It is still pre-eminently a market town for the agricultural villages round about, but of recent years other industries have sprung up, and it is now, like Chesham, a growing industrial centre.

The small market-place, which presents a busy, lively scene on Saturdays, has been made to look smaller still of late by the patriotism of Bucks people, who have crowded it with monuments and statues for which there is hardly room. The big red-brick "George," which has many memories of Disraeli, is an inn no longer, but the "King's Head," once an ecclesiastical rest-house for distinguished travellers, goes on from century to century. It has a fine stone window of the 15th century.

The parish church is well set on the highest ground; its most interesting monument is that of the wife of Sir Henry Lee, of Quarrendon, on whose tomb a red rose is always set, following a custom which is said to have been observed continuously since her death in 1584.

A mile or so from Aylesbury, on the road to Thame, is the

AT BRILL.

beautiful house and park of another Lee family at Hartwell, where Louis XVIII. kept his Court during his exile in this country from 1808 to 1814, and where his Queen died in 1810.

From Aylesbury the Metropolitan line goes on to Waddesdon, where on the crest of Waddesdon Hill the late Baron Ferdinand de Rothschild built himself a magnificent French chateau and laid out a glorious park. The station beyond is Quainton Road whence the Metropolitan line proceeds to its terminus at Verney Junction. Quainton Road is also the junction for Brill, a little town set in a magnificent position on a hill top, 700 ft. above sea level, and commanding the finest views in the county.

Quainton has a church rich in monuments and a set of old almshouses which almost persuade one to be a bedesman or a bedeswoman. At Grendon Underwood, according to almost contemporary legend, Shakespeare picked up some of his humour from a village constable which he used to good purpose in the " Midsummer Night's Dream." The Claydons, a group of three villages, have been associated for centuries with the Verney family; at North Marston, Sir John Shorne, squire and parson, conjured the devil into a boot; and at Winslow, a pretty little country town, King Offa is said to have had a royal palace.

LIST OF THEATRES

Published for the West End Theatre Managers, Ltd., by the Sole Advertising Agents, The Westminster Advertising Service, Ltd., Addison House, 26 Bedford St., W.C.2. Regent 8020 (6 lines)

Name.	Address.	Nearest Station.	Tel. No.
ADELPHI	Strand, W.C.2	Charing X—Strand Trafalgar Square	Gerrard 2645-8886
ALDWYCH ...	Strand, W.C.2	Leicester Square Aldwych—Holborn Covent Garden	Gerrard 3929
AMBASSADORS...	West St., Shaftesb'y Av., W.C.2	Charing Cross Leicester Square ...	Gerrard 4460
APOLLO	Shaftesbury Avenue, W.1 ...	Tottenh'm Ct.Rd. Piccadilly Circus ...	Gerr. 6970-1
COMEDY	Panton Street, S.W.1	Leicester Square Piccadilly Circus ...	Gerrard 3724 8978
COURT	Sloane Square, S.W.1 ...	Sloane Sq (Dis Rly.)	Gerrard 848
CRITERION ...	Piccadilly Circus, W.1 ...	Piccadilly Circus ...	Gerr. 3844 & Regent 3365
DALY'S	Cranbourn Street, W.C.2 ...	Leicester Square ...	Gerrard 201-2
DRURY LANE ...	Drury Lane, W.C.2	Covent Garden ...	Gerr. 2588-9
DUKE OF YORK'S	St. Martin's Lane, W.C.2 ...	Leicester Square ...	Gerrard 313
EMPIRE	Leicester Square, W.C.2	Trafalgar Square Piccadilly Circus ...	Gerrard 3527
FORTUNE	Drury Lane, W.C.2	Leicester Square Covent Garden ...	
GAIETY	Strand, W C.2	Holborn	Gerrard 2780
GARRICK	Charing Cross Road, W.C.2	Aldwych—Temple Charing X. ... Leicester Square ...	Gerr. 9513-4
GLOBE	Shaftesbury Avenue, W.1 ...	Trafalgar Square Piccadilly Circus ...	Gerr. 8724-5
HAYMARKET ...	Haymarket, S.W.1	Leicester Square Piccadilly Circus ...	Regent 6030
HIPPODROME ...	Cranbourn Street, W.C.2 ...	Trafalgar Square Leicester Square ...	Gerrard 650
HIS MAJESTY'S ...	Haymarket, S.W.1	Piccadilly Circus ...	Gerrard 606
KINGSWAY ...	Great Queen Street, W.C.2 ...	Trafalgar Square Holborn	Gerrard 4032
LITTLE	John Street, Adelphi, W.C.2	British Museum Charing X.—Strand	Regent 2401-2
LONDON PAVILION	Piccadilly Circus, W.1 ...	Trafalgar Square Piccadilly Circus ...	Gerrard 704-5
LYCEUM	Strand, W.C.2.	Covent Garden ...	Gerrard 7617
LYRIC	Shaftesbury Avenue, W.1 ...	Aldwych—Temple Charing X. ... Piccadilly Circus ...	Gerrard 3687
NEW	St. Martin's Lane, W.C.2 ...	Leicester Square Leicester Square ...	Regent 4466
NEW OXFORD ...	Oxford Street, W.1	Charing Cross Trafalgar Square Tottenham Ct. Rd.	Mus. 1740-1
PALACE	Shaftesbury Avenue, W.1 ...	Leicester Square ... Piccadilly Circus Tottenham Ct. Rd.	Gerrard 6834
PLAYHOUSE ...	Charing Cross, W.C.2 ...	Charing Cross ...	Gerrard 3970
PRINCE OF WALES	Coventry Street, W.1 ...	Piccadilly Circus ...	Gerrard 7482
PRINCE'S	Shaftesbury Avenue, W.C.2 ...	Tottenham Ct. Rd. Holborn	Gerr 3400-1
QUEEN'S	Shaftesbury Avenue, W.1 ...	Covent Garden Piccadilly Circus ...	Gerrard 9437
REGENT	King's Cross, N.W.1	Leicester Square King's X—Euston	Museum 3180
ROYALTY	Dean Street, W.1	Piccadilly Circus ... Tottenh'm Ct.Rd.	Gerrard 3855
SAVOY	Strand, W.C.2	Aldwych—Temple Strand—Char. X.	Gerr. 3366-7
SHAFTESBURY ...	Shaftesbury Avenue, W.1 ...	Leicester Square ... Piccadilly Circus	Gerrard 6666
ST. JAMES' ...	King Street, S.W.1	Dover Street ... Piccadilly Circus	Gerrard 3903
ST. MARTIN'S ...	West St., Shaftesb'y Av., W.C.2	Leicester Square ...	Gerrard 1243-3416
STRAND	Strand, W.C.2	Covent Garden ... Aldwych-Temple	Gerrard 3830
VAUDEVILLE ...	Strand, W.C.2	Trafalgar Square... Charing Cross	Gerrard 3815
WINTER GARDEN	Drury Lane, W.C.2	Covent Garden ... British Museum Holborn	Gerrard 416
WYNDHAM'S ...	Charing Cross Road, W.C.2	Leicester Square ...	Regent 3028-9

For particulars of current Productions see OFFICIAL THEATRE GUIDE at any "METRO" or Tube Station.

LOCAL DATA OF RESIDENTIAL DISTRICTS IN "METRO-LAND."

Station.	Trains (each way) daily.	Journey time to or from Baker St.	Local Rates (in the £).	Gas. Per 1000 feet (a); per th'm (b).	Charge for Water.	Range of Rents.	Altitude (above sea level).	Subsoil.
Willesden Green	229	8 mts.	15/4	3/7(a)	7½% rate val.	£50-£150	180 ft.	Clay
Neasden & Kingsbury	205	11 „	15/4	3/7(a)	7½ „ „ „	£50-£150	127 ft.	Gravel and clay
Wembley Park	265	11½ „	9/11	11d.(b)	9 „ „ (apprx)	£55-£70	234 ft.	Clay
Preston Road	69	13 „	9/11	11d.(b)	9 „ „ „	from £45	162 ft.	„
Northwick Pk. & Kenton	59	14½ „	9/11	11d.(b)	11½ „ „ „	from £50	175 ft.	„
Harrow-on-the-Hill	140	15 „	10/-	4/1½(a)	11½ „ „ „	£40-£400	400 ft.	„
Eastcote	45	22 „	11/7	1/1(b)	7-9 „ „ „	from £40	196 ft.	Loamy clay
Ruislip	45	25 „	11/7	1/1(b)	7-9 „ „ „	from £45	168 ft.	Gravel and clay
Ickenham	42	27 „	9/4	1/1½(b)	1/7 in £ „	from £40	207 ft.	„
Hillingdon	42	29 „	13/11	1/1½(b)	1/7 in £ „	from £45	117 ft.	„
Uxbridge	45	31 „	10/8	1/1½(b)	1/7 in £ „	£40-£120	200 ft.	Chiefly gravel
Pinner	41	22 „	8/-	1/1(b)	7-9% „	from £40	163-230 ft.	Clay
Northwood	44	27 „	11/8	1/1(b)	7-9 „ „ (apprx)	£45-£250	200-450 ft.	Gravel and clay
Moor Pk. & Sandy Lodge	20	32 „	12/-	1/4½(b)	7 „ „	up to £350	380 ft.	Gravel and chalk
Rickmansworth	45	30 „	12/-	1/3(b)	7 „ „ „	£40-£120	150-270 ft.	„
ChorleyWood & Chenies	40	37 „	9/9	1/4½(b)	7½ „ „ (apprx)	£50-£120	368 ft.	„
Chalfont & Latimer	37	43 „	10/8	1/-(b)	7½ „ „ „	from £35	410 ft.	Gravel
Chesham	27	52 „	12/11	5/3(a)	5 „ „ „	£40-£60	330-526 ft.	Gravel and chalk
Amersham & Chesh'Bois	28	38 „	10/10	1/1(b)	7½-10 „ „ „	from £40	300-540 ft.	„
Great Missenden	28	47 „	10/-	1/1(b)	7 „ „ (apprx)	£45-£75	400-600 ft.	„
Wendover	26	55 „	10/9	1/5(b)	7½ „ gross val.	£35-£150	450-900 ft.	„
Aylesbury	26	67 „	14/2	1/3(b)	7½ „ „	£30-£60	275 ft.	Clay&friable rock

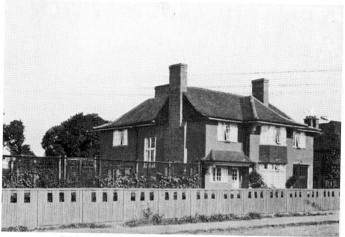

RESIDENCE ON WEMBLEY PARK ESTATE.

Country Homes in Metro-Land.

HOWEVER beautiful and healthy a country-side may be, it is unfitted for the erection of dwelling-houses until a certain amount of preparatory work has been accomplished on the land. An approved scheme, for instance, has to be laid down ; roads must be made, a drainage system planned and constructed, water, gas and electric light laid on, etc.

These preliminaries, which occupy far more thought, time and labour than appear on the surface, form part of what is termed the "development of an Estate," and have a considerable influence on its character.

It is fortunate then for their prospective purchasers that the large, new residential estates at Rickmansworth, Chorley Wood, Wembley Park, Neasden, etc., are controlled by such an organisation as the Metropolitan Railway Country Estates, Ltd., whose Board consists of several of the Directors and the General Manager of the Metropolitan Railway Company, with their experts.

A perusal of the details on the following pages will show that the skilful and experienced management, under which the Estates are being developed, is studying to combine to their fullest extent all that is beautiful in housing architecture with the natural beauties of the site.

Kingsbury Garden Village Neasden.

Situated close to Neasden & Kingsbury (Metro.) Station, about 6 miles from Baker Street, with an unexcelled service of trains occupying 10-12 minutes' journey and additional through trains morning and evening to City.
(Only one station from the British Empire Exhibition).

THE attractions of Neasden—and they are many—lie up the hill towards the cross-roads and beyond. These roads branch off towards Dollis Hill on the one hand, and down towards the Brent on the other, while beyond the Brent are the rural lanes which lead to old Kingsbury Church, near the Reservoir and Forty-lane which carries one on towards Wembley Park. Peace and quiet prevail, and the stretches of country around afford plenty of opportunity for invigorating exercise to those who incline to walking and cycling.

A Model Garden Village, at which a number of Semi-detached Residences have been erected, partially meeting the continuous demand for small houses, and all these properties have been acquired.

Well-known firms of Builders are actively continuing operations on this Estate, and Houses can be secured from £950 Freehold, with 3 bedrooms, bathroom, dining room, drawing room, kitchen, etc., and payment made on easy terms to suit a purchaser.

The attention of Builders is specially drawn to the Freehold Sites which may be acquired on payment of a small deposit and balance over a term of years. In cases the Building can be financed.

These Sites are particularly suitable for Houses eligible for the proposed Government Subsidy.

Full particulars, and a plan of the Estate, may be obtained on application to—

H. GIBSON, *Estate Agent,*

The Metropolitan Railway Country Estates, Ltd.,

General Offices: Baker Street Station, N.W.1.   Langham 1130.

A new Publication, "Homes in Metro-land," illustrating a number of Houses and Bungalows, for erection at inclusive prices, can be obtained on application to The Commercial Manager, Baker Street Station, N.W.1.—Price 2s. 6d.

RESIDENCE ON CECIL PARK ESTATE.

THE Prospective Householder who desires to fix his residence in one of the most beautiful rural country-sides to be found in all England, situated at the same time within easy reach of his business in the City, has three courses open before him :—

(1) He can acquire a site (or plot of land) amid lovely surroundings (if he chooses, on the instalment plan), either to sell over again, for the value of the plot will be constantly increasing as the locality develops, or to hold it in reserve to suit his own convenience. In buying a plot in "Metro-land," he virtually banks his money at a high (and safe) rate of interest.

(2) When he has acquired a site, he can, if he pleases, build on it. In that case, cash advances will, if he desires, be made to him towards the cost of building.

(3) He can have his House or Bungalow designed, with the accommodation he requires, by the Estate Company's Architects, and the property will be erected on a site selected by him, and an inclusive price quoted for building, fencing, Architect's Fees, and the land, and payment may be made by an agreed deposit and the balance over a period of years, as rent.

THE KINGSBURY GARDEN VILLAGE ESTATE, at Neasden, of 40 acres has been planned out on the very best garden city lines, and here small houses of different types have been erected and disposed of. Plots on this estate can be acquired on very easy terms of payment.

Wembley Park.

A beautiful RESIDENTIAL ESTATE is rapidly developing in this picturesque and healthy locality which is served by an unrivalled train service to Baker Street and the City, and linked up with the Tubes and the great Termini of London.

THE Wembley Park Estate Company are building 4 Shops immediately opposite the British Empire Exhibition at the price of £2,500 Freehold each.

There are a few Shop Plots available in the same excellent position which can be acquired on easy terms. Price from £15 to £25 per foot frontage.

The remaining Plots for the erection of Houses or Bungalows can be purchased on advantageous terms.

Further particulars of H. GIBSON, General Offices, Metropolitan Railway, Baker Street Station, N.W.1.

Telephone: Langham 1130.

A new Publication "Homes in Metro-land," illustrating a number of Houses and Bungalows, for erection at inclusive prices, can be obtained on application to The Commercial Manager, Baker Street Station, N.W.1.   Price 2s. 6d.

RESIDENCE ON CEDARS ESTATE.

THE CHALK HILL ESTATE, immediately adjoining Wembley Park Station, comprises some 123 acres, and has been planned out in $\frac{1}{4}$-acre, $\frac{1}{2}$-acre and 1-acre plots, for the erection of small houses and bungalows of a country type, with ample grounds for gardens. This is a very popular scheme of development, and a large number of buyers, are securing their plots at very reasonable prices.

THE WEMBLEY PARK ESTATE. All the houses erected by the Wembley Park Estate Company have been sold, but there is a good selection of plots, to suit purchasers' requirements, on which Houses or Bungalows can be built, and these Sites are offered on advantageous terms. Shop Sites facing the Exhibition are available.

THE CECIL PARK ESTATE and the GRANGE ESTATE, at Pinner, are the properties of the Metropolitan Railway Surplus Lands Committee, and a scheme of development is rapidly progressing. The Cecil Park Estate has a footway entrance direct from the estate on to the railway platform, and the Grange Estate, on the north side of the line, is practically touching the station.

THE CEDARS ESTATE, extending from Rickmansworth to Chorley Wood, embraces over 500 acres, a great portion of it being some 360 feet above sea level and with a subsoil of gravel and chalk. On this estate, the Metropolitan Railway Country Estates have erected detached residences standing in grounds from an acre upwards, and all these properties have been disposed of. Exceptional facilities are offered for a prospective owner to have his own House or Bungalow erected, at an inclusive cost, which can be paid by a deposit and the balance as rent.

Chalk Hill Estate,
Wembley Park.

Adjacent to Wembley Park Station, and The British Empire Exhibition in a picturesque and healthy locality, within close touch of London, yet in the open country beyond the recognised suburban area.

THIS Estate comprises over 120 acres of very fine undulating Land, with ideal surroundings including the Neasden Golf Course of 18 holes.

Freehold Building Sites of quarter-of-an-acre and upwards can be acquired for the erection of Small Houses and Bungalows, also Shop Plots close to the Station and British Empire Exhibition.

Main Drainage, Gas, Water and Electric Light Services.

Price from £175 Freehold for $\frac{1}{4}$-acre, or pro rata for larger area and £20 per foot frontage for Shop Sites.

The payment down of a deposit of £25 or more entitles the purchaser to immediate possession. The balance is payable over a term of years as rent, and the purchaser is relieved of Surveyor's charges and legal fees, the only expense in the latter direction charged being the cost of stamping documents, fees for registration and out-of-pocket disbursements.

Full particulars, and a plan of the Estate, may be obtained on application to—

H. GIBSON, *Estate Agent,*
The Metropolitan Railway Country Estates, Ltd.

General Offices: Baker Street Station, N.W.1.   Langham 1130

A new Publication, "Homes in Metro-land," illustrating a number of Houses and Bungalows, for erection at inclusive prices, can be obtained on application to The Commercial Manager, Baker Street Station, N.W.1.   Price 2s. 6d.

AT RICKMANSWORTH.

AT PINNER.

OTHER HOUSING DEVELOPMENTS.

WILLESDEN GREEN and CRICKLEWOOD.—Pleasant semi-urban neighbourhood, with practically incessant Metro. service to London. Stands 180 feet above sea level.

HOUSING DEVELOPMENTS.—On the Municipal Estate, the Brentfield, at Stonebridge, 260 medium-size houses have been erected. By private contract, about 200.

WEMBLEY PARK.—Beautiful open country. One of the healthiest spots around London. Numerous houses already built and in course of erection. Frequent Metro. service. Above sea level, 234 ft.

HOUSING DEVELOPMENT.—Municipal houses erected on Christchurch Estate, Ealing Road, 182 in number. Hundreds of other houses being built in the neighbourhood (*see* Metropolitan Railway Country Estates, pages 84 & 86 ; Park Lane Estate, page 113, and Kingsbury Hill Estate, page 111).

NORTHWICK PARK & KENTON.—Unspoiled countryside, good train service.

A large number of substantially-built houses, replete with every convenience, being erected on Northwick Estate. Charming surroundings. Well-made roads. Convenient method of house purchase (*see* pages 106, 107 and 114).

Pinner, Middlesex.

The Metropolitan Railway Surplus Lands Committee have formed New Roads with main drainage, gas, electric light and water services on the Grange Estate situate on the North side of the Metropolitan Railway line, with access to the Pinner High Street.

THERE are many beautiful sites on this Estate, and the plots have frontages of 35 feet and upwards, and can be acquired from £5 to £6 per foot frontage.

The purchase money can be paid by a deposit of £5 and the balance with interest extended over a period of years.

The restrictions and reservations include that only one house shall be built on a plot (a pair on two plots) and no house to be erected of less value than £1,000.

The few remaining plots on the Cecil Park Estate can also be secured on similar terms.

Further Particulars of H. GIBSON, General Offices, Metropolitan Railway, Baker Street Station N.W.1.

Telephone; Langham 1130

A new Publication " Homes in Metro-land," illustrating a number of Houses and Bungalows, for erection at inclusive prices, can be obtained on application to The Commercial Manager, Baker Street Station, N.W.1.   Price 2s. 6d.

AT HARROW.

HARROW.—Famous Harrow School. Growing town surrounded by picturesque rural scenery. Metro. Electric trains every few minutes to London. 400 feet above sea level.

> HOUSING DEVELOPMENTS.—Council have built a number of houses on Honeybun Estate, Bessboro' Road. Extensive building operations on Glebe, etc., Estates (*see* page 112).

EASTCOTE.—Charming rural village, direction of Uxbridge. Nearly 200 feet above sea level. 22 minutes to London.

> HOUSING DEVELOPMENTS.—Extensive housing development on Eastcote End Park Estate, situated 70 yards from Eastcote Station (*see* pages 108 and 109).

RUISLIP.—Neighbourhood of Northwood Garden City. Electric trains. 25 minutes to London.

> HOUSING DEVELOPMENTS.—Council housing scheme completed and houses occupied. Extensive private building.

ICKENHAM.—At Swakeleys, Ickenham, the charmingly-situated old-world Estate of Swakeleys is being developed as a residential estate, carefully retaining at the same time the rural beauty of the locality; numerous houses from £650 upwards are being erected. This Estate is also served by Hillingdon Station.

HILLINGDON.—At Hillingdon, in addition to the Swakeleys Estate, will be found the Halden Estate, where attractive detached houses are offered at prices from £800 upwards.

The Cedars Estate,
—Rickmansworth—
and Chorley Wood.

An exceptionally attractive RESIDENTIAL COUNTRY ESTATE, comprising over 500 acres of beautiful undulating country, rising to an altitude of over 300 feet, with a subsoil of gravel and chalk, and adjoining the old-Country world Town of Rickmansworth and extending westwards to Chorley Wood.

THE Estate is being developed for the erection of Detached Residences of the Country House type, and Bungalows of artistic design, each property having an acre or more of land, thus securing unusual amenities in this unique scheme of development.

Wide and Well-made Roads afford frontages to a few remaining Plots with a direct southern aspect and lovely views, and these capital sites are available from £650 per acre, with others in select positions up to £800 per acre. An unattached portion of the Estate, adjoining Chorley Wood Common, offers smaller Plots of ½ and ¾ acres at £500 per acre. Smaller Plots 50ft. by 150ft. can be acquired on south side of the line at £200 per Plot.

Specially Designed Detached Residences have been erected on the Estate which now forms one of the best class residential areas in Hertfordshire, and all these properties have been disposed of. Arrangements have been made for the Estates Company to build to the requirements of a prospective owner on a selected Plot at an inclusive cost for the Land, Building, Fencing, Architect's Fees. etc., and a system of purchase of the Houses (or a Site only, upon which an Owner can himself build), has been established whereby payment may be made over a period of years, as rent.

Full particulars of the Estate may be obtained on application to—

H. GIBSON, *Estate Agent,*

The Metropolitan Railway Country Estates, Ltd.

General Offices : Baker Street Station, N.W.1.   Langham 1130.
Local Office :   -   -   **Chorley Wood Road, Rickmansworth.**
Telephone : Rickmansworth 182.

A new Publication, "Homes in Metro-land," illustrating a number of Houses and Bungalows, for erection at inclusive prices, can be obtained on application to The Commercial Manager, Baker Street Station, N.W.1.   Price 2s. 6d.

UXBRIDGE.—Metro. Electric train terminus.
> HOUSING DEVELOPMENTS.—130 houses already erected. Further 450 houses planned in neighbouring districts.

PINNER.—Housing schemes (Hendon R.D.C.). Houses already built at Hooking Green Bridge and Pinner Hill Road. A number being built privately. (*See* also Metropolitan Railway Surplus Lands Committee's Estates, page 90).

NORTHWOOD.—Great Garden City and favourite high-class residential locality. Extremely healthy.
> HOUSING DEVELOPMENTS.—Council houses completed and occupied. Number being built privately.

MOOR PARK & SANDY LODGE.—Glorious spacious Park now being actively and scientifically developed as residential estate. Metropolitan Railway Station actually on estate. (See pages 104-105).

RICKMANSWORTH.—A favourite place of residence for City men. Minimum time to London, 30 minutes.
> HOUSING DEVELOPMENTS.— Urban Council have built 110 houses, Croxley Green and Mill End. (*See* also Metropolitan Railway Country Estate, page 92).

CHORLEY WOOD & CHENIES.—Chiltern Hills, and fascinating scenery. Minimum time to London, 37 minutes.
> HOUSING DEVELOPMENTS.—Chorley Wood Urban District Council have completed 36 semi-detached houses, of eight to acre. Several privately built houses available (*See* also Metropolitan Railway Country Estate, page 92, and Chorley Wood Common Estate, page 115).

CHALFONT & LATIMER. — Most beautiful neighbourhood. Above sea, 410 feet. Fast train to London, 43 minutes.
> HOUSING DEVELOPMENTS.—Conveniently situated immediately adjoining Metro. Station, numerous houses and bungalows of tasteful design and moderate cost are being erected.

CHESHAM.—Old-fashioned country town, with up-to-date municipal government. About an hour (fast service) to London.
> HOUSING DEVELOPMENTS.—Local Council have erected 120 houses and cottages.

AMERSHAM AND CHESHAM BOIS.—Composed of old and new town. Beautiful neighbourhood, about 38 minutes to London.
> HOUSING DEVELOPMENTS.—In the immediate vicinity of the Metro. Station extensive private building operations are now taking place.

GREAT MISSENDEN.—Small antique township in hollow of the Chilterns. Stands extremely high, 400 to 600 feet above sea.
> HOUSING DEVELOPMENTS.—Extensive building operations in district.

WENDOVER.—Considered the most beautiful and picturesque township in the Chilterns. Altitude, 450 to 900 feet.
> HOUSING DEVELOPMENTS.—A number of houses in course of erection in Wendover and surrounding districts.

Season Ticket Rates to and from Metro-land

From	BAKER STREET. First Class 1 Month (£ s. d.)	First Class 3 Months (£ s. d.)	Third Class 1 Month (£ s. d.)	Third Class 3 M'ths (£ s. d.)	LIVERPOOL STREET. First Class 1 Month (£ s. d.)	First Class 3 Months (£ s. d.)	Third Class 1 Month (£ s. d.)	Third Class 3 M'ths (£ s. d.)
West Hampstead	13 6	1 13 9	9 0	1 2 6	1 2 10	3 1 6	17 3	2 6 1
Kilburn	15 9	1 19 4	10 6	1 6 3	1 2 10	3 1 6	17 3	2 6 1
Willesden Green	16 6	2 1 3	11 3	1 8 1	1 8 6	3 11 3	1 1 0	2 12 6
Dollis Hill ...	18 9	2 6 10	12 9	1 11 10	1 12 7	4 1 0	1 1 9	2 15 10
Neasden	1 0 3	2 10 7	13 6	1 13 9	1 14 1	4 4 9	1 2 6	2 17 9
Wembley Park...	1 4 9	3 0 9	16 6	2 0 6	1 16 4	4 10 9	1 2 6	3 1 1
Preston Road ...	1 8 6	3 10 10	18 9	2 6 1	2 1 3	5 2 4	1 5 10	3 9 0
Northwick Park and Kenton...	1 10 0	3 15 9	19 6	2 8 9	2 3 6	5 12 6	1 5 10	3 10 6
Harrow-on-Hill	1 11 6	3 18 9	1 0 3	2 10 3	2 3 6	5 12 6	1 7 9	3 15 0
North Harrow...	1 16 0	4 10 0	1 3 3	2 17 0	2 5 9	6 3 9	1 10 0	3 18 0
West Harrow ...	1 13 9	4 4 0	1 1 9	2 14 0	2 4 3	5 17 9	1 9 3	3 16 6
Eastcote	1 18 7	4 16 9	1 5 6	3 5 3	2 12 10	6 12 0	1 16 0	4 8 10
Ruislip Manor...	1 19 4	5 0 6	1 5 6	3 7 1	2 13 7	6 16 1	1 16 9	4 10 9
Ruislip	1 19 4	5 0 6	1 5 6	3 7 1	2 13 7	6 16 1	1 16 9	4 10 9
Ickenham... ...	2 0 6	5 8 4	1 7 0	3 7 1	2 13 7	7 5 10	1 16 9	4 10 9
Hillingdon ...	2 5 0	5 14 9	1 9 3	3 15 0	2 17 9	7 13 0	1 19 0	4 19 0
Uxbridge	2 8 4	6 0 4	1 12 7	4 1 0	3 3 0	7 17 6	2 2 9	5 6 6
Pinner & E'cote	2 3 1	5 7 7	1 7 0	3 9 0	2 14 4	6 15 9	1 17 6	4 12 7
Pinner & Ruislip	2 3 1	5 7 7	1 7 0	3 10 10	2 15 1	6 19 10	1 18 3	4 14 6
Pinner	2 1 7	5 3 10	1 5 6	3 3 0	2 8 0	6 10 1	1 12 7	4 1 0
Northwood ...	2 9 1	6 2 3	1 8 6	3 10 10	2 19 3	7 7 9	1 19 4	4 18 7
Moor Park and Sandy Lodge...	2 14 0	6 15 0	1 11 6	4 1 0	3 3 0	7 19 9	1 19 9	5 2 4
Rickmansworth	2 17 9	7 8 10	1 15 7	4 10 9	3 3 9	8 13 3	2 0 1	5 8 4
Chorley Wood...	3 3 0	7 17 1	1 17 10	4 14 6	3 13 6	9 3 4	2 7 3	5 18 1
Chalfont & Lat.	3 6 4	8 5 4	2 1 3	5 2 4	3 17 3	9 13 1	2 10 7	6 6 0
Chesham	3 11 7	8 18 1	2 4 3	5 10 3	4 3 7	10 8 10	2 13 7	6 13 10
Amersham ...	3 9 9	8 14 0	2 2 9	5 6 6	4 2 1	10 4 9	2 12 1	6 10 1
Ch'sh'm & Amer.	3 14 7	9 5 7	2 5 9	5 14 0	4 6 7	10 16 4	2 15 1	6 17 7
Great Missenden	3 14 7	9 6 4	2 5 9	5 14 4	4 9 3	11 2 9	2 19 7	7 8 6
Wendover ...	4 3 7	10 8 1	2 12 10	6 12 0	4 14 1	11 15 1	3 2 7	7 16 9
Stoke Mandeville	4 6 3	11 5 4	2 19 3	7 8 6	4 17 6	12 15 9	3 3 0	8 8 9
Aylesbury ...	4 9 3	12 2 7	3 0 0	8 0 10	4 19 0	13 10 0	3 3 9	8 13 3

Season Tickets, for residential purposes only, are issued for periods of not less than three months, at half rates to all applicants under 18 years of age, provided they are in receipt of no monetary allowance whatsoever exceeding 18/- per week.

Particulars of Season Ticket Rates between other points readily supplied by the Company's Commercial Manager, Baker Street Station, N.W.1

GOLF LINKS IN METRO-LAND.

TO the City Man, the "Metro." is a short cut to the nearest Golf Course. The train service is rapid, inexpensive, and luxurious, and the districts are the most delightful adjacent to the Metropolis, being singularly beautiful, with picturesque hills, dales and woods.

NEASDEN GOLF CLUB. — A few minutes' walk from Neasden Station. 18 Holes.

WEMBLEY GOLF CLUB. — Near Wembley Park Station. 18 Holes.

HARROW GOLF CLUB.—Adjoining Preston Road Station. 18 Holes.

NORTHWICK PARK GOLF CLUB.—Adjoining Northwick Park & Kenton Station. 18 Holes and a 9-hole course for Ladies.

RUISLIP GOLF CLUB.—King's End, 5 minutes from Station. 18 Holes.

HILLINGDON GOLF CLUB.—About 1 mile from Hillingdon and Uxbridge Stations. 9 Holes.

DENHAM GOLF CLUB. — About 1¾ miles from Uxbridge Station. 18 Holes.

GRIMM'S DYKE GOLF CLUB—About 2 miles from Pinner Station. 9 Holes.

NORTHWOOD GOLF CLUB.—About ten minutes' walk from Station. 18 Holes.

SANDY LODGE GOLF CLUB.—Adjoining Moor Park & Sandy Lodge Station. 18 Holes and a 9-hole relief course.

MOOR PARK GOLF CLUB. — Adjoining Moor Park & Sandy Lodge Station. Three 18 Hole Courses.

CHORLEY WOOD GOLF CLUB.—Three minutes walk from Station. 9 Holes.

HAREWOOD DOWNS GOLF CLUB.—Nearest Station Chalfont & Latimer. 18 Holes

CHESHAM & LEYHILL GOLF CLUB—Nearest Station Chesham. 9 Holes.

EDUCATIONAL FACILITIES.

WILLESDEN GREEN. — Askes Haberdashers School ; Willesden High School ; Sunbury House Preparatory School ; Private and Council Schools.

KILBURN—BRONDESBURY. — Kilburn Grammar School ; Kilburn High School for Girls and Boys ; Private and Council Schools.

WEMBLEY PARK. — The Gables Preparatory Boys' School, Park Lane, Wembley. Good Schools for both Boys and Girls in the Town.

HARROW - ON - THE - HILL. — The Lower School (Lyon Foundation) ; Orley Farm School ; Byron Hill School ; Victoria Hall School ; St. Margaret's Girls' School ; Southlands Girls' School ; High School, College Rd. ; Harrow Technical School ; Girls' County School, Lowlands Rd. ; Boys' County School, Gayton Rd. ; etc.

RUISLIP.—Private Schools and Council Schools.

UXBRIDGE.—Middlesex County Council Secondary (higher) Schools ; St. Helen's College, Long Lane, Hillingdon ; Private and Council Schools.

PINNER.—Royal Commercial Travellers' School ; Woodridings School for Girls and Boys ; Pinner High School ; Private Schools and Council Schools.

NORTHWOOD.—Mr. Terry's School for Boys, Eastbury Road ; Northwood College ; St. Helen's Girls' School ; Temple School, Hallowell Road (Kindergarten) ; Private and Council Schools.

RICKMANSWORTH. — Joan of Arc Convent School ; Kindergarten and Boys' Preparatory School ; Council Schools, Boys and Girls also attend either Harrow, Northwood or Watford Schools.

CHORLEY WOOD AND CHENIES.—Preparatory Schools and Council Schools. Amersham Grammar School within easy reach by railway.

CHESHAM.—Private Schools, Chesham Preparatory School, and Council Schools. Amersham Grammar School 1½ miles distant.

AMERSHAM. — Amersham Grammar School ; Private and Council Schools. Amersham and Chesham Commercial College ; Turret House, Collegiate School.

GREAT MISSENDEN.—Private and Council Schools, Boys also attend Amersham and Aylesbury Grammar Schools.

AYLESBURY. — Aylesbury Grammar School ; Private and Council Schools.

Country Apartments, Etc.

NAME AND ADDRESS.	Bed-rooms	Sitting rooms	Dist'nce from Station.	REMARKS.
WILLESDEN GREEN and CRICKLEWOOD Mrs. Norton, 6 Blenheim Gardens, Cricklewood.	2	Use of	1 min.	Quiet, comfortable, large garden ; terms mod. ; board as desired.
HARROW Mrs. Hands, "Shirley," 12 Kenton Road, Harrow-on-Hill.	4	2	3 mins.	Paying guests, furnished rooms. Week ends. Lib. treat. 'Phone.
Mrs. L. Rayner, " The Cedars," 39 Bessborough Road, Harrow.	5	3	—	Bath, gar. : detached private house. Close Met. and Gt. Central.
EASTCOTE Miss D. J. Benson, Ashtree Cottage, Eastcote, Middlesex.	4	2	1 mile	Well recommended. Good garden. Terms moderate.
NORTHWOOD Mrs. Rowell, " Haytor." Chester Road, Northwood, Middlesex.	1 or 2	1	3 mins.	Good pos., bracing air, charming country. Kindly enclose st. env.
Miss Amery, " South Lawn," 16 Chester Road, Northwood.	5	2	5 mins.	Quiet comfortable home, good cooking, nice garden, terms moderate.
RICKMANSWORTH Mrs. C. Sear, "Heatherdene," Croxley Green.	3 or 4	2	1 mile	Good cooking and attendance, bath ; close to Green.
Miss E. A. Turner, Old Tannery House, Rickmansworth.	5	—	¾ mile	Boarding House and Tea Gardens. Week-end visitors.
CHORLEY WOOD & CHENIES Miss Angus, "Clovelly," Haddon Rd., Chorley Wood.	3	2	About 10 mins.	Bracing, charming country, well situated, comfortable house.
Mrs. Horace Wearing, 43 Bulls Land Terrace, Heronsgate Road.	1 or 2	1	20 mins.	High, healthy, garden opens to farm, meadows and woods.
CHESHAM Mrs. A. Rickett, Shantock Farm, Bovingdon, Chesham.	4	1	3½ miles	Ideal situation, piano, outdoor sanitation ; moderate terms.
James Walker, " Black Horse," Waterside, Chesham.	2	1	1 mile	Comfortable, good cooking. Overlooking River Chess.
Mrs. Smith, Five Bells, Tyler's Hill, near Chesham.	—	—	1¼ miles	Beautiful dist., nr. Golf Links, good cookg., comf. home, mod. terms.
Mrs. H. Batchelor, Fair View, Hivings Hill, Chesham.	1	1	15 mins	High and healthy position, bath (h. and c.).
AMERSHAM & CHESHAM BOIS The Misses Sage, Orchard House, Chesham Bois Common.	2 or 3	1 or 2	¾ mile	Well fur., good cook., bath, elec. light. gar. ; suit City gentleman.
Messrs. Rice & Blackmore, Ye Olde Griffin Hotel, Amersham.	—	—	15 mins.	Terms mod., ex. accom., week-end visitors. Large parties cat'd for.
The Misses Mayers, "Morwenstow" Chestnut Lane, Amersh'm-on-Hill.	2	1	About ½ mile	Quiet, comf., good cooking and attendance. Near Common.
W. H. Clifton, Red Lion, Little Missenden, Amersham.	3	1	2 miles	Quiet, comfortable, splendid view, terms moderate ; trains met.
GREAT MISSENDEN Mrs. Meason, " Avenold," Prestwood, Gt. Missenden.	1	1	1¼ miles	Quiet, comf., gard., summer-house, wireless, week-ends ; mod. terms.
Mrs. A. J. Ellis, South Heath, Gt. Missenden, Bucks.	2	—	½ mile	Board res., lovely view, high sit., bracing air ; very mod. charges.
Mrs. Rance, Prestwood, Gt. Missenden.	1 or 2	1	1½ miles	Large garden, lawn. Board opt. Terms moderate.
WENDOVER Mrs. Judd, Beechwood Bungalow nr. " The Leather Bottle," Wendover.	2	1	1 mile	Comf. furnished aparts. with board. Terms moderate, excellent refs.

Country Apartments, Etc.

Note.—The nearest Stations to the addresses given are shown in bold headlines.

NAME AND ADDRESS.	Bed-rooms	Sitting rooms	Dist'nce from Station.	REMARKS.
WENDOVER—contd.				
Mrs. F. Wilson, "Araluen," Wendover, Bucks.	13	—	3 mins.	Home comfs., good cook., glorious views ; 'phone 42 ; mod. terms.
Miss F. J. Morton, 4 Chiltern Rd., Wendover, Bucks.	4	2	5 mins.	Chiltern Hills, beautiful country ; bd. res. or apart., good cooking.
Mrs. Chaplin, "Courida," Dunsmoor, Wendover.	9	—	1¾ miles	Board res., on Chilterns. 800 ft. Gar. Tennis. Phone Wend'r 71.
Mrs. Thornhill, Woodside Bungalow, Little London, Wendover.	6	1	2 miles	Chiltern Hills. Splen. views, quiet, comf., liberal board ; terms mod.
AYLESBURY				
Mrs. W. Simonds, Weedon, near Aylesbury, Bucks.	2	1	3½ miles	Large gard. : small parties catered for except Sundays ; write terms.
GRANBOROUGH ROAD				
Mrs. S. Norman, Post Office, Granboro', Winslow, Bucks.	1	1 Private	1½ miles	Excel. cooking ; pony-trap, piano, bath ; good refs. ; farm produce.
BRILL				
Miss Ada E. Smith, Nashville, Brill.	9	3	1 mile	Very high, healthy and bracing. Board residence only.
Miss Badrick, "The Nest," Cross Roads, Brill, Bucks.	3	1	15 mins.	Quiet, comf., splendid views, good pos.. healthy. Board opt. Stamp.
Mrs. Butler, The Square, Brill, Bucks.	2	1	10 mins.	Comfortable, large garden, splendid views, shops ; terms moderate.

List of Hotels, Caterers, &c.

HARROW—Roxborough Hotel.

Two minutes from Metro. Station. New Lounge and Tea Gardens now open. Hot luncheons served at 1 o'clock each day. Garage. Phone : Harrow 1084.

PROPRIETOR ... ... S. VICTOR BAILEY.

HARROW—West Hill Residential Hotel.

(Off Byron Hill Road), situated in private road, beautifully furnished. Lovely old-world garden. Excellent cuisine and service. 20 bedrooms. Send for tariff booklet.

HARROW—Gayton Rooms.

Station Road. Accommodation 200. For public and private assemblies. Luncheons, teas, dinners. Phone 121.

PROPRIETOR ... ... J. WRIGHT COOPER.

SOUTH HARROW—The Paddocks.

Large parties catered for. Seating accommodation for 3,000. Extensive private grounds. Phone Harrow 173.

PROPRIETOR ... ... A. B. CHAMPNISS.

EASTCOTE—The Pavilion.

Specially designed and arranged for School and other Parties. Extensive accommodation seating 3,000 under cover. Large playing fields.

PROPRIETOR ... ... A. E. BAYLY.

EASTCOTE—Ship Inn and Pavilion.

Accommodation 300. Beautiful tea gardens. Luncheons, dinners, teas. Phone: Pinner 114. Dancing in open-fronted pavilion Wednesdays and Thursdays. Full orchestra.

PROPRIETOR ... ... A. E. FARLEY.

RUISLIP—The Orchard Bungalow.

Private Residential Hotel in an orchard and adjoins golf course. Telephone ; garage ; electric light. Seven mins. from Metro. Station. Non-residents catered for.

MANAGERESS ... ... MRS. H. G. JAMES.

RUISLIP—Fabb's Restaurant.

Residential. Excellent cooking and service. Vintage wines. Table d'Hôte Luncheons and Dinners. Tea Garden. Accom. for 100. Garage. Metro. 3 min. Popular prices.

PROPRIETOR ... ... BASIL FABB.

List of Hotels, Caterers, &c.

UXBRIDGE—Cooper's Luncheon & Tea Rooms.

Near Market House. Accommodation for 100. Every comfort. Moderate charges.

PROPRIETOR ... . FRANK COOPER.

PINNER—Ye Cocoa Tree.

The Ideal Pleasure Resort. Spacious hall accommodation for 150. Licensed for music and dancing. Luncheons and teas. Noted for home-made cakes.

PROPRIETOR ... ... J. W. CLAYTON.

NORTHWOOD—"The True Lover's Knot" Hotel.

Fully licensed. 8 minutes from Station. Luncheons and teas. Licensed music and dancing. Pavilion seating 150. Common and Golf Links.

PROPRIETOR ... ... ALEXANDER WISHART.

RICKMANSWORTH—Howe's Tea Rooms.

Excellent accommodation for Parties and Rambling Clubs up to 70. Luncheons and teas.

PROPRIETORS ... ... C. H. HOWE & SON.

RICKMANSWORTH—Victoria Hotel.

First-class Residential. Select Parties catered for. Lovely Gardens, Golf Links, Fishing. Phone: 24 Rickmansworth.

PROPRIETOR : ... ... H. W. DOUGLAS.

RICKMANSWORTH—Red Spider Tea Rooms.

1 & 3 Church Street. Luncheons, teas and light refreshments. Home-made cakes and chocolates. Excellent accommodation for parties. Open on Sundays.

PROPRIETOR ... ... A. W. WOOLLARD.

CHORLEY WOOD—The Hotel.

First-class residential, situate in ideal country, adjoining Station and Golf Links. Electric light throughout. Phone : 5 Chorley Wood.

PROPRIETRESS ... ... MRS. A. A. GRIMMER.

CHORLEY WOOD—The Green Dragon, Flaunden.

Situated in beautiful country village. Luncheons and teas provided. Boarders taken. Parties catered for. 3 miles from Chorley Wood & Chenies or Chalfont & Latimer Stations.

PROPRIETRESS ... ... E. J. TERRY.

List of Hotels, Caterers, &c.

CHALFONT ST. GILES.

Large garden. Room for 150 in garden for tea. Home-made cakes. Private sitting-room, 4 bedrooms, bathroom.

PROPRIETOR ... ... E. STACEY.

CHALFONT & LATIMER—Merlin's Cave Hotel.

Visitors to Chalfont St. Giles afforded excellent accom. Luncheons, teas. Parties catered for. Cars. Phone: 14.

PROPRIETOR ... ... H. J. ASTLES.

CHESHAM—The Gresham Temperance Hotel.

Next to G.P.O.; two minutes Station. Luncheons, dinners, afternoon teas. Lovely garden, bowling green, garage. Home comforts; terms moderate.

PROPRIETRESS ... ... MRS. M. CHILTON.

AMERSHAM—Crown Hotel (Trust House).

An Inn favoured by artists, with a delightful courtyard and inglenook. Connected in local legend with Queen Elizabeth. Good bedroom accommodation, excellent cooking and service. Telephone 60.

AMERSHAM—Ye Olde Griffin Hotel.

Tel. Amersham 75. Motorists, tourists and large parties catered for. Accommodation 100. Large Garage, petrol.

PROPRIETORS ... ... RICE & BLACKMORE.

AMERSHAM—Station Hotel.

Good accommodation. Parties up to 40 catered for. Teas, etc. Motors and chars-a-bancs, etc., for hire.

PROPRIETOR ... ... C. IVINS.

GREAT MISSENDEN—Buckingham Arms Hotel.

An old-world Hostelry, established 1631. Visitors received on inclusive weekly or daily terms. Table d'hôte luncheon on Sundays. AFTERNOON TEA SERVED—Winter: In the Oak Lounge; Summer: In the Old Courtyard Garden. SPECIAL FEATURES—Good English catering; vintage wines; personal supervision and attention. Five minutes from Metro. and G.C. Station. See advert., p. 102.

PROPRIETOR ... ... A. BRUCE BROWN.

GREAT MISSENDEN—The Polecat, Prestwood.

An old-fashioned wayside Inn. Chiltern Hills, 600 ft. Accommodation for small parties. Tea Gardens. Motor 'bus service from Metro. Station (2 miles). Fully licensed.

PROPRIETOR ... ... F. TANTON.

List of Hotels, Caterers, &c.

GREAT MISSENDEN—Red Lion Hotel.

Residential Hotel.   Beanfeast and private parties catered for.
Large dining hall.   Billiards.   Terms mod.   Cars for hire.
Phone, 71.

PROPRIETORS ... ... W. & V. J. LACEY.

GREAT MISSENDEN—White Lion Hotel.

Luncheons, teas.   Small parties catered for.   Garage
adjoining Station.   Open and closed cars, chars-a-bancs,
brakes for hire.   Private lock-ups.   Phone, No. 8.

PROPRIETOR ... ... G. OAKES.

WENDOVER—"Araluen" Private Hotel.

And Boarding Establishment.   Foot of Hills.   Glorious
scenery.   3 mins. station.   Excellent cuisine.   Tennis.
Special winter terms.   Phone, 42.

PROPRIETRESS ... ... MRS. F. WILSON.

WENDOVER—Bell Hotel, Aston Clinton.

Residential Family Hotel, amid delightful Chiltern Hills.
Fully licensed.   Tennis.   Excellent cooking.   Phone :
3Y4 Tring.

PROPRIETOR ... ... G. GLADDING.

AYLESBURY—Bugle Hotel, Hartwell.

Residential Hotel.   Spacious Tea Gardens.   Beanfeast
parties catered for.   Trains met by order.

PROPRIETOR ... ... E. STRANKS.

THE OAK LOUNGE, BUCKINGHAM ARMS HOTEL, GT. MISSENDEN.

EMPIRE EXHIBITION.

When you have explored its wonders, when its crowds weary you,
THEN think of GREAT MISSENDEN
with its enchanting hills and dells, beech woods and sylvan glades, AND

ITS OLD-WORLD HOSTELRY

THE BUCKINGHAM ARMS HOTEL

(Dating from the 16th Century).

Within whose walls ROBERT LOUIS STEVENSON sketched out
"TREASURE ISLAND," and wrote of "Beechy Bucks." Where in
the Old Coaching Days KING GEORGE III. and His Grace of
Buckingham sojourned and feasted. Where the retinue of JOHN
HAMPDEN, THE PATRIOT, rested before the fateful battle of
Chalgrove Field ; and where **TO-DAY AWAIT YOU**

THE BEST OF ENGLISH FARE

GOOD BEDROOMS & EFFICIENT SERVICE

A SHADY GARDEN for AFTERNOON TEA

LUNCHEON or DINNER on your MOTOR RUN

For an Ideal Country Holiday, stop at—

THE BUCKINGHAM ARMS HOTEL, GREAT MISSENDEN

(5 minutes from Station). Tariff on application to Proprietor.

MOOR PARK
Residential Estate

Within 30 minutes of Baker Street & Marylebone

CHOICE BUILDING SITES
Immediately available

THREE GOLF COURSES
High altitude, Gravel soil
Scenery of rare Beauty
Protected Development

Personal inspection always welcomed
Full particulars from Estate Office
Moor Park, Rickmansworth.

MOOR PARK
Residential Estate

Beautifully Wooded Heights
PROTECTED
DEVELOPMENT
Three 18 Hole Golf Courses.
Hard & Grass Tennis Courts.
Delightful Country Club.

Particulars of Choice Freehold Building Sites from
The Estate Office. The Club House. Moor Park
and the Principal Agents.

THE NORTHWICK ESTATE
NORTHWICK PARK & KENTON

LONDON'S NEW SUBURB

9 miles from the Marble Arch.
14 minutes from Baker Street.
Served by three Electric Railways.
Over 100 Trains each way every day.

A UNIQUE SPECIMEN OF TOWN PLANNING

The Largest and best laid out Estate near London.

Delightful & Artistic Freehold Houses for Sale

Each a distinctive Ideal Home in every sense of the word.
Splendidly built, only the best material being used.
Perfect rural surroundings, Lovely views, Extraordinarily healthy.
Well constructed Roads.   Main Drainage.   Electric Light and Gas,
and Colne Valley Water.

WOODCOCK HILL LANE.

THE NORTHWICK ESTATE

NORTHWICK PARK & KENTON
A New and Exclusive Residential District

A PROSPECT TOWARDS STANMORE.

A FEATURE OF THE ESTATE is the fact that **Unusually large Gardens** are provided, the average depth allowed elsewhere for the modern house and garden is 115 to 120 feet, whereas here the minimum depth is 170 feet; the density of houses per acre including roads and open spaces being about 4·5, whereas on most estates developed by modern builders the density averages from 12 to 15.

Property on this Estate cannot depreciate in value.

"THE PALAESTRA"

The Estate Recreation Ground of 5 acres in extent, laid out by the Permanent Hard Tennis Court Co., provides both Hard and Grass Courts, Bowling Green and Children's Playground. The picturesque Club House provides first-class dressing accommodation, Tea Lounge, Concert and Dance Room.

Illustrated brochure and plans and specifications of houses may be had from the Surveyors to Lord Northwick's Trust Estates :

MESSRS. NICHOLAS,
4 ALBANY COURT YARD, PICCADILLY, W.1.
Telephone - - REGENT 293 & 3377

. . . and . . .

THE NORTHWICK ESTATE OFFICE,
KENTON RD., NORTHWICK PARK, Nr. HARROW
Telephone - - HARROW 1031

Eastcote End Park Estate,

EASTCOTE

THE IDEAL RESIDENTIAL SUBURB.

EMBRACE the opportunity now within your reach of securing your IDEAL HOME amid SURROUND-INGS OF UNSURPASSED NATURAL BEAUTY.

We have here, SITUATION, ARCHITECTURE, WORKMANSHIP, ECONOMY and FINISH to suit every requirement.

This Estate is within 70 yards of Eastcote Station, $12\frac{1}{4}$ miles from Baker Street on the Uxbridge line.

There is a frequent train service to Baker Street with its connections. You can reach Wembley Park in 13 min., Baker Street 22 min. and Charing X in 36 min.

Harrow with its schools for juveniles is in quite close proximity.

IDEAL fully and semi-detached freehold villas with every convenience, built in spacious grounds are now for sale ready for immediate occupation.

Here you can have your own Tennis Court, Bowling Green and Garage.

Gas, Water and Electricity are at your door. Good metalled roads are already made.

If you desire we can build to your own ideas and design.

Experts are available to advise you on any matter. Mortgages can be arranged.

No would-be owner need fear disappointment.

We have a lifetime's experience in the building trade and are certain we can give you satisfaction.

NO AGENTS.   *Apply direct to :*

TELLING BROS., Ltd.

ESTATE OFFICE, EASTCOTE STATION.

Telephone : PINNER 210.   *Now read "Eastcote" Article on page 45.*

EASTCOTE END PARK ESTATE

A PAIR OF SEMI-DETACHED HOUSES ON OUR ESTATE.

We have varied types ready for disposal

TELLING BROS., Ltd.

ESTATE OFFICE, EASTCOTE STATION.

Telephone : PINNER 210.

APPLICANTS for HOUSES & LAND

IN

HARROW
HARROW WEALD
KENTON
PINNER
WEALDSTONE
WEMBLEY PARK
KINGSBURY

are invited to APPLY to—

Horace J Hewlitt
F.S.I., F.A.I.

Specialist in Estate Development and Sales by Private Treaty.

KINGSBURY HILL ESTATE
(BLACKBIRD FARM)

Few minutes from Wembley Park Station, whence 10 minutes to Baker Street. General Bus Service No. 8B passes Estate.

A beautiful residential estate of over 100 acres, situated amidst charming rural scenery yet less than 6 miles from Marble Arch.

FREEHOLD BUILDING SITES available at £4 10s. per ft. frontage.
ABSOLUTE TITLE. FREE CONVEYANCE.

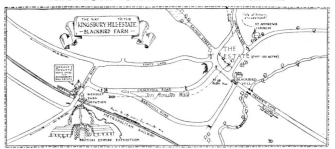

BUNGALOW & VILLA RESIDENCES from £750 to £3,000

Designed and erected to purchasers' requirements on easy terms of payment. Sewer, Water, Gas and Electric Light.

Apply to Freeholder & Builder— *Sole Agent & Surveyor—*

C. W. B. SIMMONDS

69 EXETER ROAD
CRICKLEWOOD, N.W.2.

Phone -   -   -   Willesden ONE.

HORACE J. HEWLITT

Queen's Park Stn. Phone Maida Vale 1010.
Wealdstone Station - Phone Harrow 773.
Kenton Station - Phone Harrow 994.
Hatch End Station - Phone Hatch End 149.
Wembley Park Stn. Phone Wembley 1707

111

GLEBE ESTATE. ROXBOROUGH ESTATE.
HOOKING GREEN ESTATE.

SEMI-DETACHED Brick-Built Villas on this Estate, ideally situated within 3 minutes of North Harrow, 5 minutes West Harrow Stations. Train journey about 16 minutes Baker Street or Marylebone.

3 Bedroom Semi-Det. Houses from **£750** to **£875**.

4   ,,   ,,   ,,   ,,   **£950** ,, **£1050**.

REPAYMENTS AS RENT.

Over 12 Years 19s. 11d.⎫ per Month for each
  ,, 15 ,, 17s. 2d. ⎭ £100 advanced.

Ordinary Mortgages arranged. Repayment £12 10s. per quarter, plus interest. £200 down, balance as rent.

Electric Light, Large Gardens, Pinner Parish, Decorations to suit Purchasers. Rates 8s. in the £ per year.

A. CUTLER, *Builder,*

Estate Office, Pinner Road, North Harrow.

Phone—Harrow 139.

Park Lane Estate, Wembley Park

HOUSES ON PARK LANE ESTATE.

WHY NOT live in the bracing air and rural delights of this beautiful and healthy suburb. This charming Residential Estate—nearly 200 feet above sea level—gives extensive views of a well-wooded and gently undulating countryside and adjoins Wembley's beautiful Public Park.

The Park Lane Estate is planned and developed on the best Garden Suburb lines, with semi-detached Houses to suit all tastes and requirements.

3 Bedroom Houses from **£750** to **£1,000**
4   ,,   ,,   ,, **£1,100** ,, **£1,250**

FREEHOLD or LEASEHOLD. Semi-detached with facilities for Garage.

Special Points : Sound Construction, Perfect Sanitation, Pleasing Design, Artistic Decoration.

Over 1,000 of these Houses built and sold by us at Wembley. Close to Golf Links and Tennis Courts. Low Rates, 9/- per ann. Mortgages arranged if required. Five minutes from Wembley Park Station (Metro. Rly.). Cheap Season Tickets.

COMBEN & WAKELING,

Telephone: 1656-7 WEMBLEY.   **52 Park Lane, Wembley Hill.**

HARROW and KENTON.
The House "De Luxe."
IT ONLY NEEDS INSPECTION TO APPRECIATE ITS SUPERIORITY.

£1,150 Freehold to £2,500 Freehold
£950 Leasehold to £2,250 Leasehold
SPECIAL FACILITIES FOR EASY PAYMENTS

DESIGNED for Comfort, Convenience and Economical upkeep. Hall, 2 Reception Rooms, 3, 4 and 5 Bedrooms, combined and separate Kitchens. Bathroom and Scullery Walls Tiled, and all modern improvements. Good Cupboard accommodation. Large Gardens. Room for Garage with every house.

Reinforced Foundations.
Solid walls throughout, no Lath and Plaster.
Two New Stations on the Estate.
Expresses, City (25 mins.) & West End (15 mins.).
Few minutes best Shopping Centre.
Rates 4/6 half-year.
Water, Gas and Electric Light laid on.

CAN BE VIEWED AT ANY TIME.

Golf Links and Sports Grounds adjoin Estate.
Offices :
F. & C. COSTIN, Dept. "G," Builders & Owners, Station Rd., Harrow.
PHONE : HARROW 1100 & 1101.

The Chorley Wood Common Estate

(Half-hour train journey Baker Street and Marylebone).

Gravel Soil. Bracing Air (400 ft. above sea level). Beautiful Country. GOLF, Fishing, Shooting, Boating and Hunting, all available.

DETACHED RESIDENCES (as illustrated) *already erected*, soundly built of brick (cavity walls). Entrance Hall, 2 Reception Rooms, 3 Bedrooms, Bath, Kitchen, Scullery, etc. Company's water & gas. Electric light on part of the estate. Over ½ acre of ground, well wooded.

FREEHOLD   -   **£1450**

FREEHOLD PLOTS for Sale from ½ acre. Plans of proposed Houses to be approved by the Company.

Full particulars, including Deferred Payment Scheme, from

ECONOMIC ESTATES, LTD. Phone: GERRARD 8863

56 ST. JAMES' STREET, LONDON, S.W.1.

or from

Messrs. ERNEST OWERS, LTD., The Hampstead Estate Offices, West Hampstead (Met.) Station, N.W.6.

Messrs. JAMES STYLES & WHITLOCK, St. James' Place, S.W.1.

Messrs. J. W. MORLEY & CO., 268 Earl's Court Road.

Messrs. MORLANDS, Council Chambers, Rickmansworth.

Messrs. SWANNELL & SLY, High Street, Rickmansworth.

For

COUNTRY HOUSES, ESTATES, TOWN HOUSES, FLATS,

CONSULT

WARING & GILLOW

Estate Agents & Auctioneers.

❧

VALUATIONS for PROBATE, MORTGAGE, FIRE INSURANCE, ETC.

❧

FURNITURE & PROPERTY SALES

conducted in town or country.

❧

WARING & GILLOW Ltd.

Furnishers & Decorators to H.M. the King.

164–180 OXFORD STREET, LONDON, W.1.

Telephone : Museum 5000.

Let Waring and Gillow
Furnish and Equip your Home

FOR those who wish to Furnish and Equip their Home in the Waring & Gillow style we have arranged three comprehensive schemes amounting to £300, £550 and £850 respectively. Every single item of these three schemes can now be seen in the Waring & Gillow Galleries.

DINING ROOM IN £300 HOUSE.

Carriage Paid to any Railway Station in the United Kingdom.

You can purchase Waring & Gillow's Furniture by deferred payments if you wish. Details gladly sent on request.

WARING & GILLOW LTD

Furnishers & Decorators to H.M. the King.

164-180 OXFORD ST., LONDON W.
Telephone: MUSEUM 5000
And at MANCHESTER and LIVERPOOL

We have prepared brochures giving illustrations in colour and details of the rooms in the three schemes A copy will be sent post free on request

Modern Labour Savers
-for-
Modern Homes

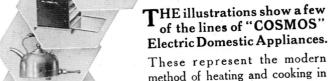

THE illustrations show a few of the lines of "COSMOS" Electric Domestic Appliances.

These represent the modern method of heating and cooking in the home. They are excellent both in Electrical design and workmanship, and are attractive in appearance.

"COSMOS" Lamps are obtainable from all Electrical Contractors, Retailers, Stores, etc., and are manufactured at their Brimsdown Works by the

Cosmos
ELECTRIC
DOMESTIC APPLIANCES

London Showroom:
232-3 High Holborn, W.C.1

METROPOLITAN Vickers
ELECTRICAL CO. LTD
TRAFFORD PARK ∴ MANCHESTER

Build your Wireless Set with—

RADIOBRIX

SR
010

MADAME TUSSAUD'S EXHIBITION

ADJOINING   BAKER   STREET   STATION

No visit to London is complete with-
out seeing the World-famous
Madame Tussaud's Exhibition.
Instructive, amusing, unique.
Maximum pleasure at
minimum expense.
Delightful music.
Refreshments
at lowest
prices.
∵

REACHED BY BUS, TUBE AND TRAIN

G.2 377/30,000.